M5S STRATEGIC MARKETING

Attract More Clients – Make More Sales

Peter Rollings

10-10-10
Publishing

M5S Strategic Marketing
Attract More Clients – Make More Sales

Published by:
10-10-10 Publishing
Markham, Ontario

Contents

*"The greatest danger for most of us is not
that our aim is too high and we miss it.
Rather, it's that we aim too low and we reach it."*

~Michelangelo~

*Dedicated with love to my kids,
Rhiannon, Katherine, and James.*

Foreword

Peter's M5S strategy is like mining for precious metals or diamonds. Get your equipment and your knowledge ready, use the internet to find your ideal clients (diamonds) and build your business to help them. You will witness a seemingly magical transformation when you make the choice to open your mind and your heart with belief. Believe in yourself, and in what you can achieve.

This book is about far more than just business. It's about designing and creating a business that works within your life. It is about how to take your knowledge and services and create something new, that is low risk and with potentially very high reward. The beautiful thing is, once you have the knowledge and the skills, you have them forever.

Peter has taken very advanced marketing information that is not common knowledge and transformed it into easy-to-take steps. He is clear that this is not an internet get-rich-quick scheme. But if you can learn and implement these steps, the rewards can be tremendous. The steps Peter shares can break you out from the shackles of fighting to make a living, and create a business you love. He shares stories that make you think, "Why not me?"

Read this book, study it, look between the lines and think about the messages he has shared. I highly encourage you to do the exercises in the 'M5S Strategic Marketing' system. At the same time and ask yourself, "What can you accomplish in the next 30 days?"

I highly recommend Peter and the M5S Strategic Marketing System!

Raymond Aaron
New York Times Bestselling Author

Acknowledgments

To my friend, Raymond Aaron: Your enthusiasm is contagious and welcome, especially in times like these. Your direction and the way you encouraged me to get this book written, finally allowed me to get this out of my head. There is so much more to come, and I thank you from the bottom of my heart.

To Mike Dillard: When you ran the group, Live Free and Prosper a few years ago, you opened my eyes to possibilities through the power of words. I did spend many years searching down rabbit holes, but I'm eternally grateful. Thank you.

To Gulliver Giles and Leila Cosgrove: You probably don't remember, Gulliver, but the conversation we had several years ago truly opened my eyes to other opportunities and the coaching world. Thank you from the bottom of my heart.

To Kerwin Rae, thank you for creating one of the most powerful and enlightening courses that I've ever had the pleasure of enjoying. Even on the other side of the world, your impact is felt. Thank you.

There are so many other entrepreneurs that I cannot even list them all here. Russell Brunson, Frank Kern, Jeff Walker, Joe Polish, Dan Sullivan, Ben Settle, Ryan Diess, Robert Kiyosaki, Christian Michelson, Bob Proctor, Tony Robbins—from courses to events, to phone calls and your free content...thank you. There are so many others that are changing people's lives and producing results in so many areas, I only can hope that I can create a small impact helping others succeed. Thank you.

To Karen Lefrancois: My most amazing sister. Thank you and Scott for the love and hospitality you have always shared. With your challenges throughout your life you are truly the strongest person I know.

To Jack Rollings: Brother, from back when we were kids, we just seem to always clash. Is there perhaps a bit of stubbornness in both of us? Love you.

To Jeff Kingsbury: The guy with the huge heart that was always there when needed and not even expected, thank you from the bottom of my heart. From a steak dinner and tequila shots when a laugh and a great friend were most needed. To writing this book in the Covid lockdown days...thanks brother.

For everyone else I know or have known throughout my life. Thanks for the love, memories, laughs, tears and lessons learned from all of you. Life has always been an adventure... keep it interesting as long as you can.

Chapter 1

Mindset – There's a Lot of Crap Going on in There

The 8 Key Questions You Should Finally Ask Yourself

————————

"Believe you can and you're halfway there."
~Theodore Roosevelt~

————————

Mindset: *the power of our beliefs and convictions, in both the conscious and subconscious minds, that provides the ultimate power for achievement and success and lack thereof.*

Hi I'm Peter Rollings,

I think it's important to know a little bit more about me and why I decided to write this book. The world is changing so fast right now. As a result ofCovid-19 and the current economy, there are a lot of people scared out there. People are worried about their jobs, their businesses, and even just going and seeing friends or family has become a concern.

Before we get any further I have another disclaimer.

The online world is filled with people selling business opportunities and how to get rich quick. There are a lot of scams, very poor programs and, well, it can be a pretty sleazy world. I have invested in a few programs that were not what I was expecting, and I was truly disappointed.

Yet every course had a nugget or two that I learned from. However, there are a select few that are exceptional.

I want to be clear, this is work. If you see anybody saying it is easy, frankly they are lying to you. Pictures of guys or gals in fancy cars, private jets and them proclaiming it is so easy anyone can do it, move on fast.

These are the people that give online marketing a bad name. That said, there are a few people that do own jets and do own the fancy cars, and did the work to make it 'easier' for themselves; they are the exception and not the standard.

The next are ones that take a course and do nothing with it and say it's a scam. These folks are equally guilty.

I see some of the best people in the industry try with all their hearts to make an impact and the trolls come along out of nowhere. It's life in the online space, these are the folks that live in negativity and chances are, unless they somehow have an awakening, they will remain there.

Here is the next thing: most will do nothing with the information I provide in this book, and for that I am truly sorry. I have tried to lay it out in a logical sequence so you can understand the opportunity and potential.

The truth is many do not have the ambition or drive to move forward. If you read this book, at the very least you will understand how professional business marketing works in today's online world.

This book and the bonuses are intended to open your eyes to the world of sharing your professional services. It is intended to help move you forward fast into creating valuable content for your audience and set your business up to grow.

Business marketing online is essential now; this is why I flip back and forth between online and offline throughout this book. My hope is when you read the book and you get the other free training at www.M5SMarkeing.com, you will see there are opportunities you may have never considered.

You may not believe some of the examples I share are possible, yet they are being achieved everyday. This book is intended to show you options to start or grow a business through online marketing and automated systems.

Somehow I got hardwired to believe there is another way. A way to build a foundation with an easy step by step process designed to lay your path forward just like a map.

You can also compare this to a contractor building your new home. The contractor does not swing the hammer. He gets the architects together working with you to finalize the design. Then he lays out the strategy for hiring sub trades. He hires the landscapers, the foundation people, electrical, plumbing, roofers, bathroom installers and every trade he needs to complete your house. By doing this he provides a service and gets paid. If he builds a bigger house, he gets paid more.

Throughout the rest of this book consider yourself a contractor. You're going to find a service, a business or a product. Then we will build out your plan and launch as fast as possible.

Ready?

Let's begin...Some of you may wonder how I got to the point of writing this so I need to go back a few years and tell you my story. This was in 2008 and was a conversation I had with the personal manager where I used to work. It went something like this...

"Peter, I really never thought I would say this. Peter, you're terminated, effective immediately."

"Can I go get my stuff?"

"Of course you can. Now come here and give me a hug."

Not a typical conversation when somebody has been fired after 27 years of employment. Yet everyone was on the list of people to be let go, including the personal manager. A few days previously, everyone where I worked was assembled in the local Art Center for an announcement.

The rumors had been flying for weeks.

There were two factories, and one was closing. Operations were being moved to Mexico. I volunteered to go first rather than watch the place, where I had worked since I was 18 years old, get torn apart. This was in 2008, the last crash that was bad, yet nothing like today's pandemic. No doubt, when you read this book, everything has totally changed again.

Little did I know what ups and downs I would live through over the next years that brought me to write this book. I always wanted to do something different, and I did not want the rest of my life to be spent behind the walls of working for someone else. There was no way I could quit to go after my goals—that job provided me with everything, and a pretty good income. The closure gave me my chance, and I went forward full out. I had a plan when the company closed, and I was excited to be free, and determined to go after my dreams. I started my own company, got into real estate, learned how to code websites, and slowly and steadily, over the next few years, got into tremendous trouble financially.

There is a lot more to the story, but my entire life, up to 2008, was controlled 100% by the company I worked for.

After I got into real estate, I discovered that there are so many things, and I heard so many stories that the average person will never hear or will never understand. The cost to some people, from making a poor decision, is enormous.

The easiest way for me to explain this is by your mortgage, which is derived from a French term that was used in Britain in the Middle Ages, and means "Death Pledge." I love working with clients, yet this wasn't the ideal way I had planned.

Something was eating away at me; I kept thinking that there is something more—a way to help more people, but I did not know the course, strategy, or even the impact I wanted to create.

I started a company with only an idea and a business plan. I built my own website that gained leads almost every day, far superior to the one that I had paid thousands of dollars for.

At trade shows that I attended (with great friends helping), there were crowds of people standing around me, listening to the story of the business, the pitch, and the plan. I had the interest. Now I needed money, and a lot of it.

I had hired Tom (can't say his last name for privacy), one of the top consultants in the industry, to help me get this business off the ground. At this time, I was looking for a private investor, and the backing in tranches (stages) of around $1,000,000.

Tom knew a few people that may be interested, and told me to take my 40-page business plan and convert it to a one-pager. "You're bothering a millionaire over their morning bowl of Cheerios before their golf game; keep it simple." I tried this for a while, and then said to hell with it, and blew the plan up to a far more aggressive idea.

In 2009, armed with that business plan, I was invited to a venture capital firm, on the 18th floor of Bay Street in Toronto, to pitch for $5,000,000. The world was still in turmoil from the crash. Yet VC firms still had millions to invest in the right opportunity.

For the next hour, I presented the company and my idea to two guys on the other side of the table. These guys typically never looked at deals that small; they financed $50 million or higher, yet these were different times.

I went home and told my ex-girlfriend about what happened. I was still excited and yet totally freaked out. She didn't think that they would ever go for the idea. In a few days, I got a call from Nick, the head VC. "Peter, we love the idea; get the rest of your proposal and documentation to us ASAP."

Holy crap!

For the next few days, I assembled the rest of the information and sent it off. The following week, I got another call from Nick. "Hey Peter, what are you asking for here?" Hesitating, I blurted out, "$5.2 million," with a huge lump my throat.

"Peter, our minimum funding is $10,000,000."

"Huh? Where did this come from, Nick? Everything we discussed was about $5,000,000."

"Yeah, it just got changed, Peter. It's no problem; we still love the idea—just double it."

Well, this was a problem, and this was when it all started: "Are you crazy?" "Everyone thinks you're nuts." "Why can't you just get a job and live the simple life?" My ex-girlfriend totally changed. Later, she did state this: "I was afraid you would leave me behind."

Well, a few years later, she left me behind, and it threw me into depths I never expected. Depression is one thing that nothing in life ever prepares you for. I got it bad; I was crushed and really didn't give a damn for or about anything for the longest time.. I never did submit the additional paperwork, and to this day, I regret it.

So here is a lesson for those in a relationship. Make sure you are both on the same page and have the same goals. A very successful guy just posted something similar to this online. He split from his wife because their goals and ambitions were so far apart.

Communication and getting on the same page is so important. I didn't fall into the booze or anything (well, not too bad); I just kept learning more, to keep my mind occupied.

I had one problem, and the problem has never gone away. There is a line from the movie, *Inception,* starring Leonardo DiCaprio. He played the character, Cobb, which sums it up. It amazes me how profound this statement actually is.

"What is the most resilient parasite? A bacteria? A virus? An intestinal worm?"

After stating this, he continues: "An idea. Resilient... highly contagious. Once an idea has taken hold of the brain, it's almost impossible to eradicate. An idea that is fully formed—fully understood—that sticks; right in there somewhere."

Once understood, you can never shake the "idea." You may shift, pivot, or change direction, but once formed, it's there for good. I will never know if I would have received the funding; however, it did open my eyes to one thing.

There is a lot of money out there looking for a place to invest. It was another world that I had just discovered. A world that I did not come from and somehow stumbled upon. This world is so far removed from working for a living and an hourly wage, for the average person it is seemingly incomprehensible.

As you're about to see, this idea got planted and has not gone away. I admit I held back on sharing what I know because the seeds of doubt kept creeping into my head. I just kept learning, investing more and more into myself in learning what I am about to share.

Many of us have the mindset that money is evil, being rich is evil, and that money doesn't grow on trees—whatever false beliefs you have had, as I did when I was younger, they have to be broken. This has been ingrained in us. I remember my parents fighting; I remember fighting many times with my ex.

The problem is that most folks have an "evil" feeling about money. There are sayings like, "Money doesn't grow on trees," "tax the rich," "money is the root of all evil," and so many more.

Then there is the voice in the background, whispering in our minds. Doubt, disbelief, and sarcasm that someone says, can be repeated constantly in your mind when trying something new, and that could change your life.

We have all been thrust into the world's biggest shift.

Everyone has gone digital. From governments, schools, small businesses, big businesses, friends and family—all are shifting to the digital world. Others are discovering social media, and the tools and systems that are connected and are overflowing with people from all over the world.

You're playing on the internet, perhaps spending hours and hours on social media.

Is it time to learn how to make money from it?

Is this the time to make a shift in your life and go after your dreams?

Are you happy in your job?

Have you ever dreamed of starting something new?

Do you have experience or knowledge that could help people right now?

Do you have a hobby that you love, and that someone else is making money from?

I am concerned that many will look back when this is over, with regret on what they could have done or should have done, but never took action.

A few years ago, the online marketing world was upended because of a guy by the name of John Reese. It is often compared to another world event that occurred back in 1954. Again, there was someone else that upended beliefs around the world, and his name was Roger Bannister. For thousands of years, it was believed impossible to break the 4-minute mile. On the 6th of May, 1954, Roger Bannister shocked the world by completing a one-mile race in 3 minutes and 59.4 seconds.

Once it was proven that it could be done, it took only 46 days for his record to be broken. The secret was out, and 24 more people did it in the following year. It was the change in belief—the impossible was now possible.

John Reese did not break the 4-minute mile.. He created a product called "Traffic Secrets," and began his build-up for a launch. On August 17, 2004, and in less than 24 hours, he reached the milestone of 1000 sales of a $1,000 product. He became credited as the first person to make $1,000,000 online in 24 hours.

I want to be clear: Don't be under the illusion that this is easy or that you can make a million in 24 hours—ever. Like starting a brick and mortar business, it takes work to get things operational.

However, just having a $100 product, and being able to sell 5–10 every week, is life changing.

When I help clients—and this is the key—they own the assets they create, and they own the knowledge forever. In many cases, this is about building a "low risk, cash flow positive business."

With all the people that you can reach in the online world, you can increase the amount of sales simply by marketing to more people. If local, you can expand your marketing, as well as the type and variety of products you sell.

This is about marketing a business online, and sales, yet it's not only that. If there is something that so many people need right now, it is a mindset shift, if they are open to receiving it.

An anchor in your mind, like in a ship, can hold your mind in one state or revert back to a feeling of positivity. Words such as *the economy*, and *Coronavirus*, are also words that can trigger stimuli that can anchor or bring a feeling back. In the movie, Leonardo used a kid's spinning top to ensure that he was living in reality.

An anchor is simply a trigger that will allow you to bring back an emotional state or belief: The sight, smell, and taste of your favorite delicious meal; a feeling that comes over you when you hear a song; the feeling you get in the pit of your stomach when you see police car lights behind you; or the feeling when you have closed a great deal.

Good and bad, these examples will typically cause an emotional reaction. You cannot help it. It is instinctual and automatic.

How does this happen?

If you are exposed to a form of stimulus through more than one of your senses, such as words, smell, visual, touch, or sight, the two become linked neurotically. Now consider this. What kind of reaction do you have to words such as *Covid-19*, *rich people*, *taxes*, *Mark Zuckerberg*, or *a breakup?* How about *love*, or *I hate him/her*, etc.?

Your feelings and ideas are the anchors in your beliefs.

Where is the anchoring coming from? Are you being pummeled by the news, conspiracy theories, your friends, or even your family?

Each of us—everyone—has the power to accept or reject what is forced onto us.

This includes the fear that has permeated every aspect of our society now. You have the choice to accept or reject the ideas and stories that you hear.

You have a choice to create your own anchor. This doesn't mean reject the dangers that are out there. It is to move forward with a positive mindset.

What if you could start with your mind clear of doubts, disbeliefs, pre-conceived notions, fear, and dread—what would this mean to your life?

What if you could wipe away all of your pre-conditioned programming and go back to a childlike curiosity? Your mind simply opens up and listens to other possibilities, and you think, "What if I could?"

There are strategies that help you remember positive emotions. Using only a couple of senses can create a more powerful emotion in your anchor.

The M5S Strategy is for business owners, entrepreneurs, service providers, coaches, consultants, and those who have a burning desire to change and take control of their future. Each part of the M5S process becomes interwoven, building on each other to *drive potential clients* to a central point...your business.

It's kind of like a clockwork system: 1–6 o'clock is getting clear on mindset, opportunity, and the first steps to get your knowledge to access the library. These become your gifts to help folks that resonate with your message and services.

The next steps, S5, is assembling the gears of the clock in place and winding it up. At 12 o'clock, you see the results, and you now can refine and adjust toward a predictable income and business growth.

Just before the pandemic, I met my publisher, Raymond Aaron, at his event in Toronto, Canada. The lockdown gave me the time to pivot and finally get this stuff out of my head. I hope to help a few folks overcome the adversity that so many of us are dealing with right now. Make a plan, and work on steps toward building and creating a future that at this time may be impossible to see.

Right now, I should pivot to a story.

This is a true hillbilly story that you can find on YouTube. Ben is standing barefoot on a deck, wearing overalls and smoking a cigarette. He looks into the camera and says, "I told you I'd be back; I'm back, and I'm still sucking on the same cigarette. Ya'll can see I'm nothing fancy, as you can tell. I'm barefoot in overalls, and I have a story that I just hope inspires you."

He goes on, "Okay, I am a skeptic; it's even says so on the back of my truck. But here's the deal. I have a third grade education, and it was the four hardest years of my life. I just did my thing; I sold hot dogs on the side of the road, and then I started teaching people how to sell them, and I was just teaching them for free."

Ben had been making a living from selling hot dogs for years. He started making YouTube videos and then started building hot dog carts with a friend.

He goes on, "My best friend's an engineer, and at the time, in 07, when the housing market crashed, we partnered up. We started building hot dog carts; he runs the plant, and I run the e-mails. I was like, "Oh yeah, I got this. Damn, I figured out how to do this. I can do this, and I know just enough to be dangerous."

Ben had also written a small e-book that he gave away, all about the business of cooking and selling hot dogs.

He then says, "Everybody has a book inside of them—that's what they say—and I already had a book. I mean, because this is the hot dog niche, and you can imagine how big a demand it is, about the same size as pooper scoopers or something."

One day, he was searching the internet and discovered a guy who is widely respected as one of the world's best marketers, and Ben was told to "take a chapter out of your book and make a mini course and sell it."

Ben said, "I already give it away for free."

He was then told, "It doesn't matter. People will buy it; in fact, more people will buy it than when you gave it away for free, because now it has value."

Ben followed the instructions and, within 45 days, made $53,000. "I was like, oh my God, from a little bitty niche." In a year and two days, he had sold his mini-course to 1,858 customers, and made $111,500.

He followed a system to deliver his course, and it's on autopilot now and still making money. This is picking a niche: *the hot dog cart industry* (picture is a screen shot from the YouTube video).

Everyone sees the world through their own personal experiences and filter. Each of our realities are different at this time, yet are still often being shaped by our past experiences. Most people are making assumptions and conclusions about their friends, families, customers, and opportunities, which many times are heavily based on how others are viewing the world.

If they continue to project the same problems, the same fear, in the same scarcity, they will naturally conclude that everybody else is in the same bad situation. Making assumptions that everybody is broke, and that no one is spending any money, could be the most expensive mistake you could make.

This is so incredibly important right now. This conclusion is simply not accurate, but more importantly, it prevents people from seeing other possibilities.

There are businesses that are exploding right now and making more money than ever. There are millions of people who are stuck at home, bored and shopping online like crazy. If you continue to believe that everybody else is in a terrible situation, you're never going to be able to see the opportunity.

Setting your life and business up for the recovery can give you so much of an advantage out of the gate, while others are watching Netflix. Just because some people and businesses are suffering, it does not mean that everybody is, or that you have to.

The lottery tag line is a "hook" that almost everyone knows, "You can't win if you don't have a ticket." So many people dream of becoming an instant millionaire, and they buy lottery tickets every week. Why is it not okay to say, "I'm going to start a business?" Many people will say, "Oh is that safe? What if the business fails? Maybe you should just get a job."

As of today, with the unemployment worldwide, you can find the determination to build a business that reflects your passion.

While most people only dream, if you can help others with your service or product, you can break free from trading hours of your life for dollars. However, you can't create a business that generates leads and sales online without a different mindset.

It gets real with THE ONE FIRST SALE.

Think and Grow Rich, written nearly 100 years ago by Napoleon Hill, is widely regarded as one of the most successful business books of all time. He interviewed the 500 wealthiest people in the world at the time, and it took him 27 years to write. There is not one thing about how to make money in that book. It's about mindset. It's about psychology. It's about being respectful to people and yourself. It's about your emotions. It's about creating internal belief strategies and rules to live by, to be used every day of your life.

Many people fight the money mindset every day. A job is limited; but in business, the more people you help and serve, the more money you can make.

Provide a service that is at least equal to or worth more to your client than they are willing to pay, and load it with extra benefits. It is those with money that are able to hire folks and help people. It is those with money that can afford to make more donations to many great and worthy causes.

Friends and family may try and stop you, quite often with good intentions, yet they do not understand. This is the world I come from also. The simple truth is that it's not your fault, just like it wasn't mine.

The school system is still based on the industrial age and sending everyone off to a factory. Colleges and universities do not teach the strategies that are going to be laid out in this book. The rules have changed, and the opportunities are still in the beginning.

Money is just a transfer of energy. It's the value of that service to equal the value of the money in the transaction.

You have to change your story.

The stories we tell ourselves—we're too tall, we're too short, we're too fat or too thin, we're too old or too young...that voice constantly reinforces the negative image, again and again. Doubt, disbelief, sarcasm, and many other things are whispered constantly into your mind.

The voice can get louder when trying something new that is outside your comfort zone. If you look at the world and you see scarcity, you become blind to opportunities and to seeing the possibility of anything different occurring.

Who is that voice? You probably actually think it's you. It's not you. It's your ego. Our egos reinforce the stories we tell ourselves. You spend so much time with that voice that you think it's you. It's been your constant companion throughout your life.

The problem is, whatever it tells you can become your reality. Many of you, right now, are still thinking that it is you.

> *"I've had a great deal of troubles in my life,*
> *most of which have never happened."*
> ~Mark Twain~

Some people say that you should try to quiet the voice. Some reach the level of "unidentifying" themselves with the voice. It's not you. Gary Vanderchuck states that he "allows no voices" in his head. You won't be able to ignore it or quiet it.

You need to recognize it for what it is... simply your ego. It often leads you the wrong way. Is it holding you back from doing something you would love to do? Is it holding you in a permanent state of fear?

The question is, "How do you change the voice in your head, and the self-sabotaging thoughts from the ego?" The vast majority of the most successful people I have met, learned from and studied work on their inner voice constantly. Shamans believe and do repeated chants. Others do incantations, and many pray.

The commonality between them all is repetition, and *the big difference is energy.*

It is having the belief with all your heart, changing not only your mindset but changing your *heartset.* Mindset will help you gain the wholehearted belief that you can come out of this pandemic and start or grow your business predictably.

You can make an income from helping others, and grow a business that you enjoy. Believe not only with your head but with all your heart that you will achieve your goals.

Shifting your thoughts from negative to positive will change the filter of the world around you, and you will start seeing opportunities everywhere. Do this every day when you wake up; do it every night before you go to bed. In a couple of weeks, you will start to change your thoughts automatically.

You have to believe, without a doubt, that you can reach the goal that you make up your mind to reach.

A few may think that this sounds like manifesting, like in the movie, *The Secret.* It has many similarities, yet it is not. This is changing your mindset, from negativity to positivity. Now I will contradict myself: Yes, this is manifesting—with massive action.

Decide once and for all that you are going to take action every day.

Here is the truth. Most people reading this will not start. There are a few that will start, but life gets in the way, and you forget about it. Some start and get frustrated, and then give up.

Then there are the others that will already know and understand what I am explaining throughout this book. They have tons of experience but are in fear of launching, and are stuck in learning mode. I know from firsthand experience about all of these aspects.

The business I started, which I presented to the VCs but never launched, sucked up my money, several years of my life and, ultimately, contributed to the loss of a relationship. Funny thing is, I am still contacted by consumers every now and then to try and launch this company. I still have straggler marketing pieces on the internet.

In the following pages, and on the accompanying website, www.M5SMarketing.com, I lay out steps to create your business marketing online. I assembled these lessons from so many great entrepreneurs, and tried to keep it as simple as possible.

Many of you may not be familiar with the terms, and that's okay. Simply try to understand the simplicity and potential of the campaigns.

What if you could take your passion, your skillset, or your business, and *grow a business faster* than most people dream of?

What would it feel like—knowing that once you have the formula, you can apply the steps, which anyone can do—if you never had to worry about gaining new clients or making money again?

What would it feel like, knowing that once and for all you have cracked the *code* on how professional marketers and business owners are making money online from their marketing? Some businesses are still growing in today's economy, and there is only one thing stopping you...and that is you.

Grab a piece of paper, and write these questions down and what you believe.

Do you have these beliefs, questions, or thoughts?

- The economy is crashing everywhere; people don't have any money to spend.

- Things are only going to get worse.

- No one wants to buy my stuff, or any stuff right now.

- No one has a use for any of my services.

- This is a horrible time to start a new business.

Write these 5 points down and, with determination, cross them out each time, saying, "This is not true."

Then write down what you want to happen.

- Write down what you *are* going to create.

- Write down what you want to feel.

- Write down what you want to experience.

It doesn't matter how *crazy* those thoughts might seem right now. Read these to yourself, with energy and passion. This needs to be done REPEATEDLY, with enough INTENSITY.

Be sure to get the bonuses at www.M5SMarketing.com. There are more resources being added all the time.

Chapter 2

Market – Local or Global – Your Ideal Clients Discovering You

4 Little Known Strategies to Attract Your Best Clients

————————

*"If you believe it will work out, you'll see opportunities.
If you believe it won't, you will see obstacles."*
~Wayne Dwyer~

————————

A few years ago, I was sitting at the computer, like so many are now, wasting time on Facebook™. I was scrolling away, and this quiz popped up: "Who is a famous British entrepreneur?" It was laid out like the game *Hangman* that kids play in school.

I answered back, "Richard Branson, the guy Gulliver's ignoring."

Next thing you know, I got a message: "Hey, want to do a quick Skype call?"

Honestly, I was shocked, but I answered right away: "Sure, absolutely."

The next thing you know, I'm on Skype with this guy from the other side of the world. He and his wife are regarded as top sales trainers and have trained many of the world's best marketers.

In their coaching program, they get groups of approximately 20 people in a room, for three or four days. After a couple of days, they all get on the phone. Yes, picking up the phone and dialing.

Their clients learn how to sell their own high ticket business packages, and training for sales—completed over the phone. *High ticket* is typically anything over $5,000. In that room, their students typically reach over a million dollars in sales. Their business is booming right now.

How do they do it?

In the beginning, each person must have the psychology and mindset training. They are trained and helped with the scripts for their respective businesses. Then they hit the phones. Yes, many of the students are scared to pick up the phone and start dialing.

They gained clarity with the training, and gained a fierce determination to push themselves forward. They also paid a hell of a lot of money to be in that room. The students invested in themselves to learn a proven system, with a goal of creating a different life.

Gulliver and I chatted for a while. He was asking me a variety of questions. Then he said, "What would you tell yourself 10 years ago? What could you say to your old self that will help you move toward your goals faster? Are there specific steps that you would tell yourself?

"Someone that thinks like you, is the easiest client to reach, to speak to, and to get them to know, like, and trust you. Help them with their problems, gain direction, or show them steps to their goals."

It's kind of like a roadmap, like the Wizard of Oz and following the yellow brick road. He planted a seed in my mind about a world I didn't know really existed.

There was something else that was eye opening about Gulliver's call with me. A couple of months before our call, he and his wife were on Nectar Island, working with Richard Branson.

This made me truly understand how close we all are to almost anyone in the world. In today's digital economy, you are really just one contact away from someone that can totally give your life a different direction.

There were a few lessons he left me with:

- Create your marketing to speak to one person, your ideal client, known as your Avatar.

- You do not need a massive idea; sometimes they are so simple, it's ironic.

- Invest in yourself, and believe in yourself.

- If you are the most ambitious person in the room, you are in the wrong room. Get around people that are playing this game of business and life at another level.

When I started my first company, and having no business experience, I went to the local Chamber of Commerce and local business experts looking for advice. When I asked about marketing, the lady handed me a 1-inch stack of paper, and said, "Your marketing plan needs to be the size of your business plan."

Here are a few stats (these are US stats; check for your own country pre-pandemic):

- 82% of small business failures are due to issues with cash flow. (Visual Capitalist 2017)

- 42% of small businesses fail because there's no market for their product or service, and 14% fail because they ignore their customers. (Visual Capitalist 2017)

- 66% of small business owners are personally responsible for three or more of the following areas: operations, marketing, resources, and product development. (Salesforce 2017)

In another city I lived in, there was what was called a Business Accelerator. The Accelerator's business model is renting office space to start-up businesses. You can network and work with other people within the building to assist you. Sometimes, if the fit is right, you can hire the other businesses to complete a service needed for your company.

The problem is, as the owner states, around 80% of the businesses that start in their offices ultimately fail. People come in with wonderful ideas, and leave disappointed, with their dreams crushed.

Business owners are told that marketing is all about getting a website; getting business cards; networking; going to events; cold calling; doing trade shows; putting ads in the Yellow Pages; having newspaper, magazine, billboard, and Google ads, as well as flyers; door knocking; and a never-ending variety of ways to spend money.

Local business experts do not understand the potential and power to grow a business through the power of the digital marketing world. Major advances in the digital marketing industry were created by those that were self-taught.

They spent years learning strategies and techniques. These entrepreneurs created automated marketing systems, which once set up and turned on, bring in new clients profitably every single day.

In fact, many will tell you that the strategies that are being shared in this book are impossible.

You may feel that way, yet this is being done every day. Folks from all walks of life, and from around the world, are achieving what only a few years ago, many only dreamed of.

Digital marketing has moved beyond websites and e-mail addresses. It has moved into a connection of systems and processes that allow spectacular and profitable growth in thousands of markets and industries.

Small business owners, both the ones just starting out, and others that have been in business for years, can end up going down numerous rabbit holes, looking for marketing strategies. Many discover marketing agencies that will provide the owner with a pretty website that does absolutely nothing to connect them with clients.

A pretty website does not follow a framework or a system that is strategically designed to grow a business or a company. It is quite often similar to a marketing brochure that people hand out at a trade show, which ends up in the garbage.

Another common problem is that business owners fill their websites with their egos—it's all about them: I did this; I did that; I'm good at this; I won this award; I have these letters behind my name, and this means I'm the best. When a visitor finds that the website has nothing for them except the ego about the business owner, what happens next is, "click," and the visitor is gone.

People do not care about you; they care about themselves.

What is in it for them? What is the benefit for them to stay on your site or get more information?

I learned how to code websites but became frustrated with my business website. I spent thousands to have another company build it for me, in 2008. It was a site that was designed as a brochure, which did not gain any traffic or leads at all. I take the blame for the wording; they just built me the 10-page website that I wanted.

I decided that if I was going to be able to market on the internet, I needed to learn more. Over the next few years, I spent what felt like thousands of hours, learning how to code and build keyword rich articles to gain free traffic from the search engines like Google.

This is based on SEO (Search Engine Optimization), so that visitors come to you without cost, just for typing in search terms in Google. The problem is that it takes forever to set it up, and a ton of time to get it working.

This is the long game.

I wanted to create something to help people, which could have more impact, results, and be much faster. Little did I know that this would take me on a journey that would last for years.

Shortly after my phone call with Gulliver, I took a trip to a business and marketing event, in San Diego, California. I had never before experienced the energy that people had at the event. I was sitting and talking and networking with people that were earning amazing incomes year after year.

They came from every industry, from all walks of life, and from around the world. You could talk to them, and they would spill their knowledge, trying to help and give you as much clarity as possible. They created amazing businesses from all aspects of life and in the craziest niches. Many of them ran on autopilot, gaining new leads, clients, and sales, even while we were talking.

In the stats on the previous page, there was a point that said, "42% of small businesses fail because there's no market for their product or service." Business owners need to have a long hard look at the business model, and determine if it falls into this category.

Are there competitors that are doing very well? If that's the case, what are they doing, and what are you doing wrong?

There are so many groups and places where people congregate online for various categories. A local business owner should look globally at other similar businesses. When you find a group relating to your niche or your business, ask questions. See if there is demand, or even explore the possibility of pivoting your business to another category to gain more sales. Online market research costs nothing except your time.

The most popular categories for information and services to sell online are anything to do with health, wealth, and relationships. There are thousands of subcategories underneath each of these three criteria. You can niche down to an even smaller subcategory (hotdogs/wealth), provided that there is a market for your service.

Know and understand your target market. This is also called *creating your Avatar*—your ideal client that needs your help, and with whom you would love to work. Craft your messages and marketing pieces that speak to your ideal client.

Good copy directed at someone (Avatar) attracts them to read more. Better copy gets readers to think you know their thoughts and feelings. The best copy gets them not only to read but to take action right away.

Speak to your market in their language, and make it simple to understand. Find out what other services they need help with. Change course with your business if needed. This is so you can *make offers to their specific needs* with your products and services.

At first, especially if you are local, it may come down to just picking up the phone or finding somebody that you're actually able to interview. The quick way to get a sample is to interview 6 people that you feel would be in your target demographic, with a variety of questions.

In your research for your perfect client or Avatar, a few of the questions you might want to determine are:

- Who is your perfect client? Give them a name.

- What is their gender? Their life circumstances?

- Where are they? Are they local, in your country, or somewhere else is in the world?

- What problems do they have that they would type into Google?

- Where would you find them (online groups, forums, etc.)?

- What are their goals? What are their dreams? Where do they hope to be in 3 years?

- What are the things in life that are most important to them?

- What keeps them up at night?

Start with one, your ideal client. Know exactly who you're selling to, in order to be able to deliver a message that resonates with them. Look at all your clients—present, past, and future—to formulate your plan to market your products or services.

- Knowing and understanding who your ideal customer is, your Avatar, helps you create better relationships.

- Creating your unique marketing message, which speaks directly to your potential client, can save you an enormous amount of time and money.

- You build trust by already knowing their problems, desires, wants, feelings, and deep down fears, and your customers will feel like you already know them.

- Show them how your solutions, services, or products will solve their problem, and the costs of not solving the problems.

You attract folks by giving away something of value; this is also called a lead magnet. There are numerous different types and styles. Examples are a free report, a cheat sheet, a webinar, an event, and there are so many more.

Crafting a message that speaks to your client's pain, desires, dreams, and goals, or excites them, drastically increases your chance of getting them to submit their e-mail, and to sell them something now or in the future.

When you create content that speaks to your client, do you think they would share it with friends? If you are in a B2B business, can you create a white paper report or articles that a potential business client would show to their boss?

If you keep creating new content, published on multiple platforms, and putting out new and helpful information, do you think your business reputation will grow?

Your goal when creating your content is also to connect. Go through the process of learning, and ask your clients questions.

Listen to them; answering will allow you to create more information. Share more information, and connect with more people than any of your competitors.

- Create stories that interest people. Just remember, when you are reaching out...people don't care about you...they care about themselves.

- Vulnerability may be hard, but it is powerful. How people share their failures, frustrations, fears, and past...it gives you a human aspect.

- Add a case study, videos, and testimonials to your marketing. Try to use inspiring stories; people like to be entertained.

- If you have to make up a story, however, create it like a fairy tale so that you are not representing something that never happened. Once upon a time...

Some of you are perhaps still wondering what you can do to start. Here are a few steps to making an income from something you love—the 4 key principles to follow:

- What are you the best at that can genuinely add tremendous value to someone? If you have not obtained the skillset, become obsessed with becoming a master. Remember, if it's something you love, it shouldn't be like work.

- Become so damn good at your craft that people can't ignore you.

- Select the way you will deliver your message—video, blog, podcast, webinar, or others that you prefer.

- Become so good that you have to raise your prices to meet your demand.

Each part of the M5S process becomes interwoven and builds on each other to drive potential clients to a central point: your business. Get your bonuses at www.M5SMarketing.com.

Chapter 3

Message – Your Experience Shared with the Masses

The 10-Step Process to Creating
Your Own Business Story Book Guide

————————

*"If someone offers you an amazing opportunity, but you're not
sure you can do it, say yes—then learn how to do it later."*
~Richard Branson~

————————

There was a business event in Australia a few years ago, and from this came a story about a lad from India. He went to a previous event, and he was hungry, determined, and wanted to succeed.

The following exercise was to create an e-book to be used as a lead magnet. The goal for the class was to have it published by the very next day.

The course ended for the evening, and everyone broke for dinner. He went to his room. He worked until around three in the morning and had his e-book published online that night. This was not a big book. It was a small report, around 15 pages.

It was designed to be quick, easy to read, and yet pack a powerful punch with content. Remember that today people have short attention spans and get bored easily.

The report is designed to draw them in and keep them reading. His report was on rubber and synthetic hoses for the airplane industry.

After publishing his e-book, he continued his follow-up of building his marketing process and business systems. From this report, his exposure and contacts grew. Shortly after the event, he set up a manufacturing plant in India.

He is now a major supplier for Boeing and NASA. The strategy that I am sharing is powerful, and the impact and results speak for themselves.

Another powerful example of digital marketing is Tesla. Several years ago, they completed the most successful capital raise in history, direct to the consumer. They had a simple sales funnel, and success of the strategy speaks for itself.

They were launching the Tesla Model 3, and they created a landing page that was connected to a simple three-page marketing website, also called a funnel.

Page 1- Landing Page: "Watch the unveiling of the new Tesla Model 3, live." Consumers had to sign up with their e-mail to be notified or reminded.

Page 2- E-mail System: People were notified by e-mail and were reminded to watch the live stream of the unveiling of the Model 3.

Page 3- Order Page: On the unveiling page, there was a link to pre-order the Tesla model 3, for $1,000, plus e-mails were sent out after the event.

This resulted in *$14 billion dollars in pre-orders* for the Model 3.

The Cyber Truck was also absolutely dramatic for Tesla's marketing. Elon Musk had stated that the windows were shatter-proof. At the live event, they did a test by throwing balls at the windows. The balls almost shattered the windows.

It went viral, attracting a ton of free press. This resulted in 250,000 pre-orders for the truck. These are two examples of how a simple three- page funnel, designed with automated systems, can work.

A marketing system that converts strategically and profitably can actually grow a business without any cost. When the ads are converting to sales, or when you spend one dollar on ads and you gain one dollar in income, the marketing becomes free.

These are the keys to the kingdom, when you reach the goal of sending $1 and getting more than the dollar back in direct sales. The goal is to build the one thing that you will truly own in business, and that is your e-mail list.

Your business reach and marketing potential today is unlimited. At no time in history has it been so easy to reach anyone, anywhere in the world, with the click of a few buttons.

Creating a predictable *marketing system* allows you to push your content, services, and experience through numerous channels, and allows your business to become *omnipresent* in the marketplace.

Note: By the time the vast majority of you read this, the world will have dramatically changed again. Social media today, as of May 2020, has the primary channels that people use, such as Facebook™, YouTube, Instagram, Twitter, LinkedIn, etc.

Everything is changing so fast that anything that I explain today may not be working when you read this. There may be a new platform that has revolutionized social media.

That's why this book covers the framework of creating your content and using the systems to share your message. This is so that it truly doesn't matter how you get your message out. The rules of content will still apply.

- *Facebook™ is marketing*...there are 2.45 billion active monthly users in 2020, and there are more than 1.62 active daily users.

- Mobile user growth will reach 4.68 billion in 2019; 87.4% will use a Smartphone for internet access.

- LinkedIn, YouTube, Messenger, Instagram, and Twitter are marketing channels that can reach more of your clients.

Social media is NOT just for friends and family. It is for business marketing, and now it just became essential for businesses, not only to survive but to thrive. So many people are on social media channels every day; it's kind of like being able to place your ad, your stories, and your content in front of a stadium full of people.

There are people needing your services and are waiting for you to reach out. Even if someone is not using social media, their friends and family are.

Have you ever been to the grocery store and seen the National Enquirer, or perhaps seen a Readers Digest? You scan the cover, and there's an article that is somehow drawing you in? You can't help picking it up and reading the article.

The writers are able to write stories that attract attention. Writing copy or copywriting is not about re-inventing the wheel. It is about following the path of others before you that have written successful copy.

You explore what worked, and modify it for your own business purpose. Understand that this does not mean to "copy the article"—that's illegal. It is taking professional sales letters and repurposing them in the very best way, with your spin, to use as your own.

There is a reason that it is called copywriting. When you find a successful competitor, look at the words in the copy—are they filled with benefits for the reader, with a call-to-action to find out more?

A call-to-action may be a button on the site that is asking you to provide an e-mail address. It can be summed up in one sentence: "Copywriting has a measurable action for the reader to take, that can be improved upon through repeated testing and iteration."

A professional copywriter will cost you thousands of dollars, or even tens of thousands, if you are lucky enough to find or even be able to afford a good one.

The reason is that the sales letter they create can earn hundreds of thousands of dollars, or in the right industry, millions of dollars in sales. The best in the world are in high demand, and selective about whom they work with.

"Content is king" is a saying that started a few years ago. Right now, it is much more important than before. People's attention spans have gone to less than that of a goldfish. There's so much noise and advertising to compete with that your content needs to jump out.

Your marketing needs to catch their eye, for them to read it or watch it. Make your marketing especially relevant to your market.

Somehow you need your own system for creating your perfect messages that your clients would love to read, and that is what the next part is for.

The 9 Essential Elements to Create Million Dollar Messages

I modified this title from a business coaches training, because the following was so profound in the results. Following this system makes it easier and faster to create your own personal information content bank.

Following this process will allow you to have: an e-book, a white paper report, a special report, the framework for a 10-chapter book, 10 information products, 10 titles for 10 books, 10 articles on your website, or 10 websites, an outline for a one-day seminar, 10 information products, 10 videos, 10 podcast topics, 10 press releases, a 10-step autoresponders e-mail series, multiple angles for marketing, 10 letters, 10 subjects for coaching sessions—and this is just the beginning.

When complete, this becomes a written article bank, which allows you to share more of your content with more readers. It begins simply with:

First: The title – This is the title of your e-book or report. Examples: Training Your New Lab Puppy; Essential Tax Tips for Small Business; Building Your New Dream Home; Scrapbooking to Your Heart's Content.

The top 10 things you need to know about _____.

That's it—a curiosity headline that speaks directly to the reader. The next step is planning out what you will share. What's the first thing you teach them? What is the second, the third, the fourth, through to the tenth? They can be individual titles or a sub-headline, depending on how you design the report. They are designed to arouse the reader's interest and to get them to read more.

Second: Your sub-headline – This is it—the *most important element* of your article. You have a fraction of a second to attract a potential client. It has to be bold and stand out, and interest them. If not, they're gone, and you've lost them.

Examples are:

- The 3 mistakes people make...
- The 5 keys to...
- The 4 elements...
- The 6 habits...
- The 7 underlying principles...
- The 5 questions...
- The 4 secrets...
- The 7 rules...
- The 8 reasons...
- The 10 laws...
- The 5 dangers...

Do any of these look familiar? They probably do, because they are common and because they work.

It grabs attention with a hook—the title of your article that draws people in to read more. People in your target market become more aware of you.

Third: Your first line of copy briefly needs to be interesting to draw them in. The first paragraph should have three to four sentences maximum.

Fourth: 3 to 4 bullet points of key facts, statistics, or points that you want to bring up in your article. These should be relevant—

statistics interest people, and if you need to complete research, Google it.

Fifth: Add a story that supports your case. It could be a life experience or something you've heard before. Do not make up a story that's false, unless you let them know that it's not a true story. Create several more paragraphs to get the clarity of your point across.

Sixth: You want a metaphor or simile. An example: "It's kind of like fishing. When you go fishing, you need the right tackle and bait, the right location, and the right strategy to catch the fish you're after."

Seventh: An inspirational quote from a famous person.

Eighth: A small picture or piece of art that can simply explain the story. It can even be stick figures.

Turn your business focus away from what you want, and try to answer these questions:

- How can I provide a superior service or product to meet the needs of other people or companies?

- How can I create the solutions far beyond the reach or service of anyone else to create the outcomes people or companies desire?

- What else can I do, create, or offer that increases my services so that it's almost impossible for my clients to NOT get the results they desire or want?

There's a saying that *people love to buy stuff but they hate to be sold*. If your product or service is not the best on the market, what can you do to make it better?

When business advertising predictably makes money, it transforms marketing from an *expense* into a *must-have investment*. It threatens competitors because once the process is working, companies can literally outspend their competition without limits.

When you publish your articles, you're not just giving these away. The free reports that you create are given away as a lead magnet. People opt into your e-mail list to get your magnet. This is the start of changing business marketing, and growing your e-mail database of potential future clients.

Your e-mail should have your company name, such as peter@M5Smarketing.com, and not peter@gmail.com or yahoo.com. This is basic and not hard to set up, and yet it looks so much more professional.

Another tip is to not use info@—use sales, appointments, etc., based on potential departments. It is not a major item, yet it looks more professional to that person that may become a client.

Ninth: E-mail auto-responder (an automatic mail response tool that is connected to your landing page) – People enter their e-mail to get their free report. It is built, created, and designed to send new e-mails that you pre-populated to automatically send to your list. Inside the auto-responder, they can be segregated into separate buckets or categories.

For example, a group that got your free report, and another separate group created for those that have purchased.

Your list is the only business asset that you absolutely own. Each person on your list expressed enough interest to provide you with their personal e-mail. These are folks you can keep in touch with, share more about you and your company, and sell products to.

It is widely accepted that the size of your list, or the number of people you have subscribed, represents $1 in income per month. So, for a list of 5,000 people, you have the potential of creating an income of $5,000 per month.

If you get to 10,000 people, you could create an income of $10,000, and so on. Service and industry varies. There are some industries where the value of the potential client list increases dramatically, such as real estate, both residential and commercial.

Many of you have heard of the 80/20 rule; for those that haven't, the basic explanation goes like this: It is called the Pareto Principle, and it is also known as the law of the vital few. It means that 80% of the results or effects come from 20% of the effort or causes.

In business, and including an internet business, the goal of the 80/20 rule is to find the most productive parts of your business and make them a priority. When you identify the 20% of the systems or factors that give you the best results, you will find more efficiency to create increased profits.

Direct your focus on the 20%, the clients that you make the most money from. Market specifically to them and at the same time, this will help you acquire new clients with the same characteristics. There is nothing worse than a client that sucks the life out of you.

It's the same when building your list; 80% of a company's revenue is generated by 20% of its customers. Focus on the 20% of the clients that result in 80% of your revenues, and provide more value or services. Help them more, and at the same time, increase your income.

This is about using your best asset efficiently, your knowledge and expertise, to create maximum value. For example, when you're sharing your free reports, keep an eye out for the ones that generate more leads. Can you capitalize on that "one thing," to generate more leads and more income for your business?

After all this is created, the question is how you will bring it into the world, in the most efficient and profitable way possible. In the next chapter, we cover the secrets of how powerful an individual campaign can be.

Be sure to get the bonuses and additional training at www.M5Smarketing.com.

Chapter 4

Momentum – Small Improvements to Exponential Possibilities

The Simple 8-Step Process That Has Created Millions

—————————

"Everything you've ever wanted is on the other side of fear."
~George Addair~

—————————

One afternoon, I was on Facebook™ when this ad came across my feed. I can almost remember word for word what was said: "Hey, it's Mike here, and a lot of you may have wondered where I disappeared to after leaving the multi-level marketing industry a few years ago.

Well, I've got a big announcement to make for a few of you who might be interested. I'm going to pull back the curtain to show you how I created two $25,000,000 businesses online, in this exclusive training program.

There's nothing to buy and no obligation; just click on the link to find out more." That was it, short and sweet.

Now, up to this point, I was really open-minded, but I was a skeptic. The only programs I had on investing online, were how to build websites, code, and SEO. As I already stated, these work; however, they take a lot of time.

Not only on your part, and writing continuous articles based on SEO, but also the time it takes to index on the search engines. It is a constant fight to be able to keep your articles ranked high enough that people would actually see them.

The goal of any business that is using SEO, is to get their business on the first page. This is the typical system that many business owners use. They can expand their reach with Google ads, and this can be very profitable when working correctly.

The problem is that the costs of Google ads are expensive, and if the marketing is not making money, it becomes a huge expense. Another problem is that you do not own the traffic going to your website—Google does.

Curiosity got me, and I clicked the link.

This advertising was to a cold market (I didn't know who he was) and was *designed to capture an e-mail.* Mikes was offering a one-year training at the cost of $37 a month.

On Mike's next video, he explained more about who he was and what his plan was for the group, and the benefits for everyone that joined. I listened intently to what he had to say. I was still questioning about joining.

I had never bought something like this from an ad. I kept thinking about it, and how many hours I had spent learning how to build effective marketing through websites and SEO.

There was something different about this presentation, and for only $37 a month, and with his guarantee to make me feel secure, I bought it.

On the next page, he had another video. In this, he asked people to commit for the entire year. It made sense; if I was going to commit to learning, I needed the year. This is what is called an upsell, and for $247 for the year, I was able to save a few dollars.

Honestly, I cannot remember his exact numbers, but I think around 500 people joined the one- year program, giving him an immediate cash return of $123,500. In addition, approximately, a thousand more people joined the $37 monthly program, creating a monthly revenue stream of $37,000. On the date he stated the doors were to close, he actually closed the doors, and no one else could join.

Even with 1/10 of the number of clients joining a program like this, it would drastically change people's lives, assuming 1/10 of the results would be an immediate income of $12,350, and a re-occurring revenue stream of $3,700 per month.

Rinse, improve, and repeat again. Keep in mind that this is why you should try and select something you love to do. Again, it all starts with the first sale.

It turned out that he was one of the most widely respected marketers in the industry.

Mike's marketing had an 8-step system that consisted of:

- Facebook™ ads with a short video

- A landing page with a short video

- A thank you page with another short video

- A sales page with a video, a payment processor, and a monthly membership option

- Another sales page, the upsell, with the one-year payment offer to save some money

- A thank you page, with specific directions on what consumers are to do next

- An e-mail auto-responder series

- A membership site

Everything I knew about how business marketing works—with building websites, business cards, print ads, trade shows, cold calling, and so much more—was now thrown out like "the baby with the bath water."

You can write the very best articles, have the very best product in the world, and it doesn't matter. You need to be able to reach people to let them know about you and your product. This course was my "AHA!" moment. There were so many ideas that just exploded when this realization went off.

We are truly in a global market. You truly have no limits on what you can earn. You do not have to create hundreds of articles based on keywords, and wait for the search engines. You need to create articles that are packed with a punch and that interest people.

The vast majority of websites are almost designed like a gatekeeper to keep people away from your business. They are often confusing, with far too many choices, resulting in driving your visitors away.

The secret is to create your lead magnet, combined with your hook(s), which attracts your ideal client's attention. Keep in mind that this is for both online and offline businesses.

Business and industry growth are being upended by the rapid growth of the new digital economy and the reach of professional marketing.

Marketing today uses a process and system designed to put the perfect message in front of the maximum number of potential clients possible.

With so many people on social media, your business cannot afford not to be. I am only touching on Facebook™ because costs have come down. It is the most cost effective way at this time to reach the maximum number of people. A business owner may desire to use LinkedIn; this platform requires a different strategy.

Facebook™/ Instagram ads: Learn the basics of Facebook ads, and the process. When you get to the stage of hiring somebody to look after your social media, you know exactly what you're talking about. This may also stop a few from pulling the wool over your eyes. Your strength and advantage is that you are in a far more knowledgeable position. Instagram is owned by Facebook™, and is another process to learn. Master one, then move on to the next.

Cloning yourself: Who knows your business better than anybody else in the entire world? Who is invested in your business more than yourself? Who is the best salesperson you have, other than you?

Mike created a script for his video message, and used a teleprompter just like they use for the news. It becomes clean, direct to the consumer, and you will know very quickly how well it works. This is a powerful lesson I learned from Mike: When you record your perfect message to your perfect client, it makes your life so much easier.

Landing page: Also called a squeeze page, this is not a website. The landing page needs to be simple and clean, like Apple computers.

When someone lands on the page, they have only two choices: enter their e-mail address to get the lead magnet you created, or leave. That's it; there is no other choice. It is designed with a message that resonates with the market.

Mike had a video, and he recorded himself to deliver the perfect message. Every time it played, people listened to the same message, freeing up time for him to gain sales, and for him to work or play as he desired.

The thank you page: This most valuable piece of real estate in a typical business website... is wasted. Think about this; of all the millions of websites in the world, this person somehow stumbles onto your little website, and actually leaves their e-mail. They get a "thanks for signing up; we will be in touch soon."

So now you have new hot prospect thinking about what you have just presented or offered. They may want or need what you have, right now, and your website pushed them away for another day. Chances are almost certain that they are gone, and you have lost the chance to make a sale.

Mike had a video on the thank you page. It was simply a "thank you for signing up, and look to your e-mail for further details." This did a couple of things. One, it created curiosity and anticipation about what his next message would be. Two, people had to use a real e-mail and not a phony one to get the next message. There are a few choices you can make, depending on your service or business.

Sales page: The sales page is sometimes also on the thank you page. Provide the consumer with logical benefits to sign up to work with you right away.

Upsell page: The upsell page for a business or service is a premium package that offers a definite benefit to the consumer. Mike's offer was to sign up for a year and save some money. Throughout this book, I give a few other examples of upsell pages. After every sales page, you need another thank you page, with the directions for what the consumer needs to do next. You have to spell it out, as easy as A, B, C steps, for what they are to do next. You must not leave your new subscribers or clients confused.

Mike only had a few e-mails for his entire program. His advantage was that he was a professional copywriter. He creates messages that speak to his ideal clients, which can draw his clients to him.

Membership site: There are a variety of platforms to create your own membership site. Each has their own features and benefits that can be utilized based on your business goals. One of the advantages of a membership is that it provides consistent income for online service providers.

A problem with a membership site is monthly payments. People typically drop off after the third month. You need to keep adding massive value for your clients to avoid the drop-off.

Appointment calendar: Depending on your business or service, people can book an appointment on your calendar. There are numerous tools to complete this online, as well as CRM (Customer Relationship Management) systems.

PLEASE NOTE: All e-mail systems must follow Can-Spam laws. Anyone receiving your e-mail has subscribed and has the opportunity to unsubscribe at any time. Follow the rules, because the penalties can be enormous. To make it easier for business owners, most auto-responder software companies have this feature built in. *Do not buy e-mail lists!* Build your own database of clients.

Even today, many companies do not even have an e-mail list. For those that do, quite often they don't have a strategy or a system in place to keep their clients at top of mind. At least tell stories, or share specials, events, or anything that could keep you connected with a client.

Split testing: This is the *silver bullet* of online marketing and modern marketing strategies. You are putting your visitors unknowingly through an experiment every time they visit your site.

There are two variations of your landing page running all the time. It may be a different image, different copy, different videos, or different colors; the variation could be large or be very small. This is the beginning of testing parts of your funnel.

You are searching for the combination that improves the number of people signing up, and how conversions can be improved. Conversions are the visitors that actually sign up on your landing page, and connect with you and your offer. Split testing is taking your first landing page style 'A' and then testing it automatically against 'B'; this is also known as A/B testing.

When starting out, the conversions can be quite low; more dramatic changes may be needed when experimenting. The beautiful thing is that you can actually find, and duplicate, a landing page and entire funnel (site) that somebody similar to your industry is successfully running. The key is to test, test, and test again.

For example, you run a test to each landing page 'A' and landing page 'B.' Both get an equal amount of traffic, each having 1,000 visitors. The rotation of landing pages is automated.

- If landing page 'A' has 50 (5%) conversions, and landing page 'B' has 100 (10%) conversions, landing page 'B' now becomes the control.

- Now, a new variation of landing page 'B' is created. 'B' is now called landing page 'A,' and it is tested vs. the new 'B.' Now, again, after 1000 visitors to each page, the new landing page 'A' (that was 'B' on the first test) again has 100 (10%) conversions, and the new landing page 'B' has 150 (15%) conversions. Landing page 'B' now becomes the new control. Keep testing to improve conversions.

Your landing page, your thank you page, your sales page, and any upsells and downsells are being tested constantly in your entire working funnel. The power of testing each of these continuously can dramatically increase the probability.

Split testing can also happen inside your advertising when you use Facebook™. When running ads, you can also set up multiple variables where you start scaling up your spending while still testing.

Retargeting: Have you ever been followed by an ad? This is due to a little piece of invisible code placed on your computer from the site you just visited.

This is what your business advertising should do. Google has announced that they're going to remove third-party tracking systems within a couple of years, to enhance privacy—this was called a cookie.

Facebook™ uses what's called a pixel. When you click on an advertiser's ad, and you continue to see the ads again and again, they are re-targeting you. If you see ads that you have never seen before, it may be because of what they created—something called "a look-a-like audience."

Advertisers can ask Facebook™ to look for people that are similar to the people that they were successful in getting e-mail addresses from. Can you see the power in this?

Every part of business is a numbers game that has three core principles: traffic to your website or storefront, conversion rate and sales of the people that visit, and the economics of everything to this point.

Are the systems that you as a business owner have in place, able to take the cost of traffic and conversions, and create a positive economic outcome? With each piece of the 3, what area can you improve?

I have to throw in an example of how people can reach $100,000 a year. Depending on your business model, product, or service, earning $100,000 per year in business, from professional online marketing, takes only a few paid clients.

Mike's training was based on a membership site with a cost of $37 a month; 225 paid members is $100,000 per year in income. Gaining only around 400 annual paid members, at $247, is also $100,000 per year

One Time Sales		Membership Site	
$100	1000	$37	225
$247	404	$47	177
$750	134	$97	86
$1000	100	$247	34

This lockdown is so life changing, and I hope a lot of people realize that many live so precariously. I have lived a life where my employer controlled every aspect of it—what hours I worked, when I was allowed and not allowed holidays, how much I was paid, and basically every other aspect of my life.

I also know firsthand what it's like to be let go and to struggle to find something that I truly enjoy doing.

I appreciate and understand how this feels for those of you that are there.

Look in the mirror and meet your competition.

Now let's move on to the fun part: how to make money with what you know. Please go to my website, www.M5SMarketing.com, for the bonuses and for further explanation and training.

Chapter 5

Monetization – Looking for Profit in Hidden Places

How to Steal McDonald's "Big Mac" Strategy

—————————

"Happiness is not in the mere possession of money;
it lies in the joy of achievement, in the thrill of creative effort."
~Franklin D. Roosevelt~

—————————

I've connected with so many people through business, real estate, and marketing, and there's one thing that I have realized. This game of marketing, sales, and business is a game. It can be frustrating and disappointing, just like going to work every day to a job you hate, with a bad boss. It can also be eye opening and amazing when you achieve results from your efforts.

There's a common theme that so many successful business people believe. Money is simply energy; it cannot be destroyed.

You provide value, money changes hands, and it's simply transferred from one place to another. Even at this time of the pandemic, economic crash, and massive unemployment, there are still people making money, and the internet is open for business.

If your business provides a service, or you're able to create a product that solves a problem, you charge money for it. There are a few people saying that you shouldn't be selling right now. If you are still able to help people reach their goals, solve their problems, or help them move ahead in life, why are you not allowed to make a living? You have your bills to pay, and you have to be able to feed your family.

Questions that often get asked are: "How much do you charge for your product? What kind of problem are you solving, and how much value is it worth?"

For a marriage counsellor, a question could be: "What is it worth for somebody to save a marriage?" Some people will pay almost anything if they can get the results. They don't want to go through the cost of lawyers, courts, and the crushing heartache.

What is the value of the service you provide?

This will take a mindset shift.

It is not about the information or the product that you provide. It is about creating a transformation and solving customers' problems. It is stated many times that you need to provide at least 10x the value when creating a product or course for clients. This is online marketing and swapping over to brick and mortar sales; this is the same.

A system like the M5S program is about creating or packaging up business services to expand your reach and income. The goal is to move away from trading time for money; you create packages for selection by your clients. You give away fantastic information for free.

The people that want more attention and personal service can purchase the next higher package if they desire. The same applies in numerous niches and business services. No matter your industry, you can add more value and income in your service.

Many people are not used to paying thousands of dollars, or even tens of thousands of dollars, for services, training, or coaching. Yet by not utilizing the opportunity that is being presented, if it is the right fit, chances are they will be in the same spot one year from today.

Those that realize that it is the results that they are paying for, know that it's an investment in them, their business, and for their future. The guide or coach provides a map, direction, and clarity to help them achieve the results they desire.

Most high ticket coaches realize that people paying $2,000 or under for a course are needier than those paying in excess of $10,000. Folks that pay even higher amounts, such as $30,000 or more, need even less hand holding. This can actually be for the same training.

In the world I came from, paying thousands or tens of thousands for coaching or consulting is unheard of. I paid my first consultant for my business, the one that never launched, $10,000 up front, and to this day I have never stopped investing in myself.

Jay Abraham, widely considered one of the best business coaches in the world, has a formula that simply explains why and how businesses succeed or fail. The number of clients that come to a business, times the average dollar sale amount, times the number of transactions they do per year, equals business revenue, or:

No. of Clients X Average $ Spent X No. of Transactions = Revenue

Let's make up a guy called Dave. Dave is a small business owner, has a few employees, and is selling around $600,000 in services a year.

Every year, they have 1000 clients walking through the door and spending an average of $200. With his business model, they come back, on average, 3 times a year for more purchases.

No. of Clients	Average $ Spent	No. of Transactions	Revenue
1000	200	3	$600,000 per year

When you create your Avatar, the person you would love to work with, you will know everything about Dave—his hopes, dreams, fears, and what keeps him up at night. Dave has been stuck at the same revenue for several years, and decides to revise his marketing and sales processes.

The Power of Your McDonald's Strategy

When you drive through McDonald's, and you ask for a Big Mac, what is the first thing they ask? Would you like fries with that? Next, "Would you like a coke with that? Would you like to supersize that?"

This simple question, "Would you like fries with that?" is a billion dollar upsell, and is crucial to the profit and operating margins for the franchise owners. Employees are trained to say it every time. They don't ask, "Would you like a second Big Mac?"

This is creating an offer that has a complimentary feature to the original product and makes sense to the consumer. Your goal is to increase complimentary items and services so that the intrinsic value increases for the consumer.

The packages that businesses create add additional or complementary services or products that make total sense. In these cases, the consumer may pay more; however, it may solve a few other problems they had not considered.

What does your company offer as the "Big Mac" or "the hamburger?" How can you create and package up complementary items or services before or after the hamburger? It could be a smaller front end offer that has a minimal price, yet draws additional consumers to your mailing list. It could also be an offer on the back end of your burger.

Dave realizes that his customers may be open to other items that complement the higher priced purchases typically made. On the front end, he offers a low price entry product. He finds that with this low cost product, it draws additional customers and sales.

He also adds a back end product and creates a package for a slightly better price for all combined. Dave also creates a new system for referrals at the same time. By increasing each part and the efficiency of his sales process by 10%, the revenue of Dave's company grows exponentially by around 33%.

No of Clients	Average $ Spent	No. of Transactions	Revenue
1100	220	3.3	$798,600

The numbers have a far more dramatic impact if Dave increases the amounts by 20%. This grows the company and profits by 73%.

No of Clients	Average $ Spent	No. of Transactions	Revenue
1200	240	3.6	$1,036,800

It took years for me to discover the power of incremental growth and improvements, and the powerful effect it can have on the bottom line of a company. I, like so many business owners, relied on duplicating what others in the industry are doing. If you are in business now, look at how you can improve your processes by even a small amount.

An hourly wage is the model that the vast majority of the population understands. Someone earns $20 per hour and goes to work for 40 hours per week, and they make 800 bucks, less taxes. If they want more, they can perhaps work overtime to get a bit more on their paycheck.

Perhaps they have a degree behind them, and they are on salary. Typically, the only way possible for each of them to increase their income is through a pay raise if the company desires to give one.

The other model, to increase the individual's worth to the company, is by going back to school. You probably all realize the cost of a university education, and the debt that students carry well into their adult lives. There is also the business model of meeting folks one on one for an hourly fee. In all of these examples, this is also called trading hours for dollars.

Let's assume another fictional example, of a psychologist named Jill. There is a limit to the number of clients Jill can help, as she works one on one. Jill charges $100 an hour; so, typically, she can work 7 hours a day, with an hour for lunch. The maximum she can make per week is $3,500. If she takes time off, she makes nothing. How can she change this?

There are common questions that customers ask Jill every time. Another way to think of this is perhaps frequently asked questions (FAQ). Where does Jill get this content that she can record? Remember the last chapter? She has already created a10-step outline.

The basic package Jill creates is her 90-day online program based on her core curriculum. Clients can ask questions, and she creates the responses for the benefit of the entire group.

She also offers bonus features, such as an additional online, 1-hour, live coaching session per week. She now has a commitment for a total of 16 hours to work over the next 90 days. She also adds a guarantee.

Her program is regularly priced at $100 an hour, with 10 hours of recorded sessions based on the content she already has created, with a value of $1,000.

The 16 live, online sessions, at another $100 per hour, answering her clients concerns and questions, adds another $1,600. The regular price of her basic program is now $2,600. For this package, she discounted it by 50%, to $1,300, for the 90-day program plus bonuses.

She also decides to limit the size of the group to 20 people, for scarcity and to be sure that each client can have additional time to purchase if needed.

Jill can now add personal live coaching sessions (online) in addition to the recorded sessions. Jill's services are now packaged; and now, rather than working one on one, she can work "one with many." She can experiment with different offers and packages that appeal to visitors. The maximum number of packages to create is 3; any more than that would confuse people with too much choice.

Jill's income is now $1,300 per client, after the program is created. When she fills the program with 20 clients, her income is now $32,000. She has only 4 hours of work required per week for the next 90 days, and this changes her hourly income to $2,000 per hour.

Her clients are happy because it is cheaper than her normal rate; plus, they can purchase additional coaching if they like. This is her basic package. There are two other packages she can create.

On her next level, she offers additional hours of personal counselling, with several other bonuses. Her premium package is a one-year discounted program, with many other extra features, such as a retreat. Can you see the potential for any business?

Jill's case is a simple example that I created to try to plant the "idea." This is how marketing a business can exponentially increase someone's income.

Do not be afraid to give away your best information for free. This typically happens in the marketing world.

Here are a few things to keep in mind.

You will discover haters when you start marketing online. It will not matter if you have 99 positive uplifting messages thanking you... there will be one person that can drag you down. Block them, forget them, and move on. These folks, you cannot help.

There will always be people that will never buy anything. There will always be people that can actually figure out your product and service. Perhaps they figure out how to do it themselves.

When you give free information, it also creates goodwill, and what is called reciprocity. It helps get people to know, like, and trust you. Some will now share your content or will refer your information to their friends and others. Others will buy your packages.

A few, your ideal clients, can become your brand ambassador.

Let's do another example.

Let's try the construction industry; we'll call the owner, Tom. Tom has been running a successful construction company for 25 years, and he has built hundreds of high-end custom homes and developments, with very satisfied clients.

Tom is getting older and is ready to slow down; however, he realizes that the knowledge and experience he has is extremely valuable. He decides to enter coaching and consulting to help others that want to follow in his steps.

Tom creates a training program exactly as Jill did. The difference in Tom's is that he only offers high ticket, one-on-one coaching. He is also going to be very selective of who he will work with. In this case, Tom creates two packages.

The first package is a 6-month training program for which he charges $25,000, and acceptance is by application only. He rejects more applicants than he accepts, and he charges a modest fee for even applying to his program. He is deliberately weeding out time wasters and tire kickers.

His next package includes everything in the six months, except that this is an intensive one-year personal coaching and consulting program with live support. The premium package includes far more personal attention, and a guarantee that his clients will advance years ahead in their business.

His price is $100,000, paid in advance, with a maximum of five clients only. Any other expenses he incurs are charged to the clients. Can you see the power in this model also?

Sometimes someone's knowledge can be more valuable than the actual business they are running.

A successful business owner, creating a guide and offering coaching services at the same time, can be an amazing combination. High ticket sales and coaching are booming all over the world.

If you look into your field or idea, and you see there's a lot of competition, this is an excellent sign. You know people are buying.

Generally, it does not matter that there is competition, because there is only one of you.

Your voice, your personality, your experience, and your personal touch will attract your own tribe and your own customers.

When you are entering a market, here is something else to consider. You need to create a sub-niche, or a smaller niche within a niche. If your niche is broad, such as real estate, you will be diving into a bloody red ocean, where the competition is fierce.

Creating your own sub-niche, with your own title and twist, creates what's called a blue ocean strategy, and the sub-category can become yours to take.

The truth is that hiring a professional digital marketing agency that is able to create a profitable marketing system, can be exorbitantly expensive. Here is an example of a business model used. Let's go back to Dave's company, with the company making $600,000 per year. This is not a real conversation; it would no doubt be much longer. However, the premise will explain, and the conversation may go something like this.

Dave: "Hi, I would like to hire you for our marketing, and set up your system with us."

Agency: "Sure, what are your revenues?"

Dave: "Around $600,000 per year."

Agency: "Sure thing, we can do that. Cost is $100,000."

Dave: (just about puking) "Say what?"

Agency: "Look, we can set this up to increase your profitability year after year, and you own the system. After it is operational, all we would charge is a monthly fee to maintain it; plus, we will put guarantees in place to make you feel more secure."

Dave: "I can't afford $100,000."

Agency: "OK, I get it. Lots of people can't. I have another option for you. In this case, we will set it up for $20,000; you do need to have some skin in the game. We will need to go over all operations of your business, including sales and follow-up, to make sure that you have operations and sales processes dialed in.

We establish your baseline of sales (assume $600,000 in revenue @ 20% profit) on an agreed upon amount.

Then after we set up the marketing, and new profits start coming in:

- First, you get your $20,000 back. We do not make anything until this fee is returned. Then you are not anything out of pocket.

- After the original amount is paid back, the new profits are split, 70% to you and 30% to us.

Our income is totally based on your success. How does that sound?"

Dave: "I like it; let's do it."

Here is the payback, at a 10% increase on each aspect, over the 5 years.

Year	Revenue	**Profit	Owner Payment	Agency Payment
Agency Hired	$600,000			$20,000
Year 1	$798,600	$159,720	$131,804*	$27,916
Year 2	$1,054,152	$210,830	$147,581	$63,249
Year 3	$1,416,184	$283,236	$198,265	$84,611
Year 4	$1,694,140	$338,828	$237,179	$101,649
Year 5	$2,488,416	$497,683	$348,378	$149,305
			$1,063,207	$446,730

*Year 1 – $20,000 original investment paid back
** Profit remains at 20% annually.

Each part of the process is improved, including marketing, conversions, and the number of times purchased, as explained in the previous chapter. In this example, rather than earning a one-time fee of $100,000, they have earned nearly $500,000.

Conversions and increases of each aspect of the company operations are so powerful when a marketing agency works well with a company owner, and can establish the growth in a controlled manor.

The numbers are far more dramatic in years 6 to 10. Consider if they increased the business by 20% or 30% in the first five years.

Is a few thousand dollars expensive to create a website for a company or service business? Many businesses are charged this amount per month, or more, for their marketing. Is the formula in place to create profitable marketing?

To these companies, all marketing is considered an expense and not an investment.

What is the cost to a business owner that has a disconnected marketing approach? What is the cost to a business owner researching and trying to solve the problem without help? What is the cost of fixing the issues when someone did a terrible job? How about the cost of ignoring it while everything gets worse? What would be the cost of fixing it later, if it continues to get worse?

Key points to consider:

- This agency is now almost essential to the operations of this company.

- The agency is not going to be targeting 10% growth; they will be targeting the maximum growth possible.

- What happens if the agency starts with a competitor to the company?

There are companies that charge $1,000,000 plus a share of profits to set up a professional digital marketing funnel. These are the very best of the online marketing professionals. The products and services they provide are *'predictably profitable.'*

Did this give you clarity on how a business can grow exponentially, and how any business can grow, using only the M5 part of the process? Be sure to go to www.M5Smarketing.com to get your bonuses and extra training.

Chapter 6

The Strategy of Simplicity

The Bakers Dozen – The Steps to Simple Automated Marketing

———————

"Believe in yourself. You are braver than you think, more talented than you know, and capable of more than you imagine."
~Roy T. Bennett~

———————

A story that put a lot into perspective for me was about a guy named John. One day, John was sitting at home watching TV with his wife. It was a quiet evening, and they happened to see a special report about a new hot item that people loved. He decided to do a bit of research to explore more about this "hot item."

He created a quick website, with a survey, and asked people a simple question: "What would you like to know about the hot item"?

He posted to forums that were dedicated to the new hot item, and received around 120 answers. Next, he then went online and began his search for someone to answer the questions.

In only a few days, he found and hired someone to complete the assignment. The person he hired did all the research and, in fact, wrote the entire book, answering the 120 questions.

John loaded the book onto his website, started his marketing and sales, and was selling the book for around $37 each. He still sells 2 to 3 a day, and continues to create a residual income of around $35,000 a year. John created an amazing resource that his clients loved, even though he didn't actually create it.

He made the choice to move beyond just trying to figure it out. He went directly to his target audience and asked the questions, and asked someone to do the research and to even write the entire report with all the questions and answers.

This e-book was about scrapbooking.

 John has never in his life scrapbooked, knows nothing about it, and has never even read the e-book.

There are a few lessons that you can take away from the story:

- Always keep an eye out for opportunity and what is hot on the market right now.

- A simple survey, asking people what they need, is a fast way to narrow down a product.

- Outsourcing a project can save hundreds and hundreds of hours of work.

With most training courses I did, each seemed to have only one piece of the puzzle, and the puzzle got bigger and bigger. There always seemed to be something else to learn, build, and develop.

Your mindset, belief, and the action you take in this is so important, especially in times like this. Mindset alone has had thousands of books and courses created. Tony Robbins' business is based on shifts in your mindset, and beliefs of what is possible. There is no end to the mindset training that you have access to; it's everywhere.

It's your future, with the ultimate certainty you have for yourself and the future. Everything is a mindset game, even just completing the work in this book, and the bonuses you receive at www.M5Smarketing.com.

In case you haven't figured it out, this does take work. It is not a get-rich-quick scheme. Many people fail and fail again, and keep going back for more. The mistakes they made, add to their arsenal of knowledge, and once they break through, the knowledge is owned forever.

Who Not How

Dan Sullivan is a globally respected business coach. He has a very powerful saying, which is also the title of his book, *Who Not How*.

What this means is that when you discover a task beyond your expertise, which will take a lot of time to complete, instead of asking, "*How* do I do this?" ask yourself, "*Who* can do this?"

What could take you weeks or months of work—if you ever complete the project—can be completed so much faster and more efficiently by using someone that specializes in the task you need.

With scrapbooking, it shows how even hobby-based businesses can create a terrific side income. Speed is efficiency in the online world. Again, it's not HOW you can do it, it's WHO can do it for you. Get it complete and launched, and fix and polish the little and big things later.

In each project that you want to complete, write down the key points of what you need, want to create, and why.

- What is the importance of this project, on a scale of 1 to 10?

- Every time you hit a project that is 8, 9, or 10, deal with it fast.

- If it's anything from 5 to 7, write it down on a future to-do list, and set it aside.

- Projects that are under the scale of 5, you might not deem as necessary later.

- Explore outsourcing every part of the work and services you need.

When targeting online sales, you have numerous options and a lot of tools to help. The following is a list of various types of business strategies.

The 7 Elements to Understand in Online Marketing

A Sales Funnel: It is one of the major tools of digital marketing. The name may sound odd, but this part of the process can take a business from virtually unknown to an automated million dollar marketing machine, faster than any previous marketing strategy could before.

Imagine a real funnel: At the top of the funnel, something is poured in, and it narrows down to a specific destination.

In the online world, people drive traffic from numerous sources, to the top of the funnel, or your landing page. People decide whether to enter or not; however, when they do, it becomes a multi-step process, designed to get visitors to take action and complete a purchase.

There are four basic steps in any funnel.

The first is awareness—when people first become aware of you or your product.

The second is interest—they signed up to get your lead magnet, or to find out more information about you and what you're doing and offering.

The third is decision—often, the hardest part is to get a customer to pull their credit card out.

The last part is action—this is the final stage that you want them to perform. This is also known as AIDA: attention, interest, desire, and action. The part that is missing is R—relationship—and that is what you are doing with your list and marketing, getting this part in play for future clients.

It is important to go over a few of the terms, especially for those that are not as familiar with online terminology.

E-mail autoresponders: I am repeating this because it is so important. This is an automated system designed capture prospective customer e-mails and to automatically send your e-mails to everyone on your list.

Depending on your business model, they are designed to keep your reader informed as you publish new information and, always, in a roundabout way, ask for the sale.

Direct Response Marketing: This is a sales and copywriting technique to get customers to take immediate action by opting into the offer that is presented to them. With Direct Response Marketing, an example you may be familiar with is what is called a long-form sales letter.

It quite often includes a story of a product and service that is built around the psychology of getting people to take action. They are also still common in newspapers or magazines, where you see a very long article, and it looks similar to an in-depth newspaper report.

Traditional advertising in newspapers, magazines, television, and radio are a mass market approach, and is kind of like blasting a shotgun and hoping one of the pellets hit. Direct response is a targeted approach to a specific reader or demographic, with emphasis on the words or copy of the article.

E-Commerce: This is selling products online. Perhaps some businesses that are now shut down could still be operating if they had a system and online presence. Shopify is one of the most well- known brands offering this service for individual stores. Amazon does this also; however, they just cut the commissions on resellers throughout the market. I am on a few feeds owned by e-commerce professionals that share relevant information to all industries and marketing.

Information Products: There are quite a variety of information products, and there's an endless variety of our products being launched every day. There are courses, training, information products, events, and many more, such as using Jill's business example. This book is information, and if you joined the program, you have seen firsthand the funnel in operation.

Affiliate Programs: An affiliate program is when someone else has created a product that you are able to market, sell, and share in the profits of sales. An example is when someone creates a $1,000 program or course, and you become an affiliate. You promote it through your marketing channels, and you receive 50% of the income. There are so many different varieties of affiliate programs; you need to explore this to find out more.

Membership Site: A monthly fee similar to the program I purchased from Mike. A similar program for selling physical products would be a subscription model.

One-Time Payment: Get paid all up front. It's the same model as Mike offered, with the one- year discount, and the same as the example I gave about Tom.

Low Ticket: This is often called a tripwire. A service or product is created and sold for a small fee such as $7 to, say, $47. This is typically designed to cover the cost of advertising. On the thank you page, there are often upsells to a higher priced course or other options. Remember the McDonald's strategy: "Would you like fries with that?"

High Ticket: These are courses, trainings, and coaching that carry a premium price. Typically, prices start around $2,000, and depending on the profession and the market, can have a much higher price tag. It is common with some coaches and service providers to have fees in the 5 and 6 figures.

Launches: This was created by Jeff Walker, who created Product Launch Formula. Jeff took a long-form sales letter and turned it into what he termed a "sideways sales letter." Through a series of several videos, each video building on the previous video, an offer is made to the consumers on the fourth video.

Subscription Model: This is like Mike's program, which was for one year at $37 a month.

Webinars: A powerful way to build your list. This is not like the boring PowerPoint presentations that you may have seen. Every time you run the webinar, you watch and see where people fall off (systems will do this for you). You adjust the part where people fall off, and run it again. The first few days of the week that you're promoting the webinar, you run it live and see the results.

Keep testing, and improve at some point in the future when it converts well. It can be converted later into a recording and automatic timed events, or run on demand. This is called an evergreen system. Somebody finds your business, adds their name to your database, and can watch it instantly, or at other preset times you have.

The webinar is based on psychology; it is designed to speak to your perfect client, and their hopes, dreams, and desires and you move them through a journey. There are strategies to build a webinar that can convert very well for its owner, and convert every time it is run.

With the report, you create, "The 10 things you need to know about _____; it's time to get these put into action."

If you have a webmaster, talk to them about building a landing page, and giving away your free report in exchange for an e-mail. You can search Google for "Great Landing Pages," to find examples and duplicate the look of a successful competitor's site.

Keep it simple and clean, like an Apple computer landing page.

If your webmaster does not know what you're talking about, perhaps it is time to consider hiring somebody that does. With everything that has been explained so far in this book, are they actually earning or costing you money?

My goal for this book was to try and enlighten a few folks about *the cost of not* trying to create something you love to do. If after a while it doesn't feel right, you can always change it later. Every time you attempt to complete a task, you are just simply learning the process.

Keep going back to www.M5SMrketing.com for more help and information.

The 4 basic steps to begin to build your marketing funnel are:

- Get your "10 things you need to know" report transferred into a downloadable PDF report; outsource this task if necessary. Later, as you get feedback from your clients, each part can also be expanded into a larger separate report.

- Your website landing or squeeze page, created with the headline and copy directed at your target market. Try to use every word possible to convey your message with the benefits of them providing you their e-mail.

- Your e-mail autoresponders, with pre-populated initial e-mails, to be sent to your list automatically. Begin building your list.

- Your thank you page that may say, "Thank you for signing up to get the report; it will be on its way to your inbox shortly." Then, on the same page, a video or a small sales letter that offers an option for your product or service, to your visitor immediately. You don't even have to have this to begin. Perhaps you send them to a survey or a waiting list for your launch. Create a survey and ask them questions.

This alone begins to transform your marketing to building your list. This also sets the stage for the process of getting everything into automation. The next 3 steps can include:

- Create the first duplicate (A/B testing) of your landing page with a few modifications. Have your split testing immediately operational when you launch.

- If you're selling a product or service online, you need a payment processor to accept credit cards.

- Have an appointment calendar connected to your schedule so that prospects can make appointments based on your scheduled time, if desired.

Outsourcing: Even if you have the budget, learn these systems yourself; later, if you find you need to hire someone, hire them. Just get the first part started; keep it simple yet pack a punch with your free content.

A word of caution: When you begin exploring and understanding how these systems operate, you may be led down rabbit holes left and right. Work on the one thing you need to get done, putting all your attention and focus on that one thing until it's complete or outsourced.

This is not a $20, $30, or even a $40 job anymore; the entire setup and process is about results. Be aware of the value that a professional marketing person can bring to your company, especially when they're well-versed in marketing strategies.

Each part of the process of digital marketing is tested, tested, and tested, constantly, to improve conversions and results. This is not building a website, slapping it up on the internet, and saying, "You have your marketing system."

The cool part happens when things start to come together and you see them in operation for the first time. Understanding the simplicity of getting your business launched is coming up. Be sure to visit www.M5SMarketing.com to get your bonuses and more details.

Chapter 7

Systems – Powerful Tools of the Trade

The 8 Essential Principles to Gain New Connections

—————————
*"Success is not final, failure is not fatal: it is
the courage to continue that counts."*
~Winston Churchill~
—————————

A story I love is about a JV, or a Joint Venture. JVs are basically an alliance of two or more companies, with the goal of creating a mutually complimentary outcome. This is from a business coach in Australia, and can be found on YouTube.

There was a lady who was the owner of a high-end spa, and she hired a consultant, as she desperately needed more business. They explored what she offered to her clients, and designed a very unique promotion. They approached Porsche, BMW, and Mercedes Benz, and asked if they would like to have gift baskets to provide customers.

The car dealers would give them to anyone that took the cars for a test drive. The spa owner would provide the baskets and all contents, to the dealers for free. The baskets were to be filled with shampoo products and a variety of items that were in her spa; plus, she would add a complimentary, 1-hour gift certificate for her spa. The car dealers loved the idea and, of course, they said yes.

She freaked out!

She started saying that there was no way she could afford this for potentially hundreds of baskets.

This is what the consultant did: He said, "Hang on; give me the names of all your suppliers." He called them and said, "Hi, we're doing a promotion with Porsche, BMW, and Mercedes Benz, and we were wondering if you would like to contribute some of your products for gift baskets that we are providing to them?"

The suppliers were thrilled to be doing a promotion with companies like this. Every supplier sent the spa owner their products for free, and all she had to do was add her gift certificates and buy the baskets.

The result was that people came in and loved the one-hour treatment; shortly, the spa was booked with high-end clients. The total cost for her promotion: $6 per basket.

The reason I added these stories is to give you a different perspective. Everything that I have presented is based on content and creating a marketing system. It does not have to be just about the internet. Joint ventures are one of the most powerful ways to increase exposure to a totally new audience, and for a minimal cost. A few lessons that can be learned:

- By selecting select JV partners, you can target folks or businesses that want premium products.

- You can partner with non-competing industries to gain a mutual benefit.

* The cost of promotions can be very affordable and, at the same time, very dramatic.

The rest of this chapter may be the one that many of you dread; it's been seen thousands of times before: how to build the technology side of the marketing funnel. There are a lot of you right now that have the self-limiting belief that you are not computer friendly.

In fact, many of you may be thinking that with everything that is presented in this book, there's no way you can possibly do it. Everyone, even the best in the world, started exactly where you are...at the beginning.

If this is you, are you paralyzing yourself before you even start? Let's put this aside for a second and assume that there is nothing that is going to stop you. You're damn smart and dedicated enough to push forward and figure out the few steps to be able to get your marketing system launched.

There were so many people just like you, who have made it so much easier. They also were feeling that they did not have the ability. The tools such as landing page builders are software (SAAS software as a service), and are typically available for only a few hundred bucks a month. These systems are being used in thousands of different industries, businesses, and niches.

The cool part is that you don't have to start from scratch. You find competitors in *your* industry, from anywhere in the world, using similar systems, and model exactly what they are doing. They have proven templates that you can use right away. Just modify with your copy and offer, and away you go.

In regard to creating a landing page or squeeze page, this is not coding a website. These are basically drag-and-drop editors that someone, even if they are not tech-savvy, can set up and get running very quickly.

It's step one, step two, step three, and then keep following the process and getting your gears of your marketing system in place. *Who*, not the *how*—if you are still resistant, understand the visual of what you want to create, and hire it out to someone. There will be more information at www.M5SMarketing.com.

You're not trying to reinvent the wheel. Follow a simple strategy and, at the same time, provide massive value, more than your competitors ever considered.

If you're a perfectionist, this is something that you are not going to follow. You are going to launch, get it going, and clean it up later. Speaking from experience, perfectionism leads to tremendous procrastination on getting a project done.

Your business landing page does not need to be perfect; it needs to be launched. Even absolutely horrible ugly websites/landing pages can convert incredibly well with good copy. Do not worry about creating a beautiful site.

Get the gears of your system in place and working. Before launching, you're going to test the system and make sure each aspect of it works properly. This is especially important if you are using an online payment processor. Later on, you can add other parts to the funnel, to increase the chance of engagement with new clients.

There are business owners whose landing pages convert in excess of 60%, and sometimes even higher. They are adding hundreds and hundreds of new e-mails and potential clients to their database every single day.

Help identify and give direction to solve a problem with your free content. Often, your clients learn that they have a problem that costs them money, time, or health issues, perhaps before they were aware they had one.

Sometimes it is just creating a fun thing for them to pursue, which they are willing to pay for rather than deal with the frustration of figuring it out.

The power of a system that utilizes tactics and strategies, with all processes, cannot be understated. This pandemic will end, and it's the companies that are able to adapt and offer more to customers that will come out the strongest.

There's a great book by Robert Cialdini, called *Influence*, and in this book, he outlines his six principles to move buyers through to the stage of purchasing:

The Principle of Reciprocity – This means that sometimes people feel they are obligated to give back to others because they've received a gift first. In a study, it was found that giving diners a single mint at the end of the meal, increased tips by around 3%.

Surprisingly, it was also found that if the gift was doubled, and 2 mints were provided, tips didn't double—tips went through the roof, with a 23% increase, depending on how it was given.

Principle of Scarcity – Can you build scarcity into your offer, videos, or e-mail sequence? If there is only a limited time for your offer, or only a certain amount of slots available, it entices people to take action, similar to the fictional example I created about Tom's business.

Don't play games here. I've seen a lot of people start a course, and they state the cut-off time, and then they extend it past this deadline. If you're cutting it off on a certain date, stay true to your word and cut it off.

Principle of Authority – How much authority do you or your products or services have? Do you have other respected people that you know, who could endorse it? These elements can have a tremendous effect.

Doctors establish instant credibility; the idea is that people are more likely to follow those that have credible authority. The foreword of this book is written by a *New York Times* bestselling author.

The Principle of Commitment and Consistency – Get them to commit to something, such as free shipping, or to download a report to move them into action.

Principle of Liking – When people like you and trust you, it will play a huge role in whether they decide to act on purchasing something from you. Persuasion science tells us that we like people who are similar to us, people who pay us compliments, and people who cooperate with us toward mutual goals.

Principle of Consensus – Do you have social proof? Getting people to talk about how great your products are can help tremendously with growing your reputation for your product. When people are unsure, they will look at the actions and behaviors of others to help them determine how to proceed.

There are numerous ways to get information to the world today, such as YouTube, press releases, podcasts, information products, keynote presentations, seminars, webinars, auto-responders, sales letters, white paper reports, social media, joint ventures, and so many more.

When you share your knowledge and expertise to help people, you can establish yourself as an authority in your industry. This can allow you to connect with more folks that could potentially become clients or even partners.

- Help people by sharing excellent information; you are the expert in your field and could be a solution to their exact problem, and who they are looking for.

- Relay how expediting solving their issue will allow them to move on, and the costs of not solving their problem.

- Get clear on information vs. transformation in your marketing messages. They get results in the shortest time possible.

There is a fundamental shift in strategy when it comes to marketing a business online. Traditional marketing methods, such as advertising in newspapers, going to trade shows, and meeting people, has never grown an audience.

When you're providing value through a lead magnet, and connecting through various forms of media, the goal is to actually build yourself an audience.

You ultimately want to reach the people who you are best able to help. This means marketing to your perfect client, the one person that you would love to work with every day.

When you're able to reach that one person, they can become a brand ambassador. This can create the opportunity where they share it with friends or even business associates.

Referrals and organic growth can make a huge difference in traditional industries, such as brick and mortar, not just online. Consider all of these points when you are building out your lead magnet.

Yet it is up to the individual to change or to stay where they are. They have to own it and accept responsibility for where they are in their life right now. It is 100% my fault where I am; I own it. It's 100%

your fault also, and you need to realize this and accept it. The question is, what are you going to do about it?

What is a mastermind group? Napoleon Hill, the author of *Think and Grow Rich*, wrote and taught about masterminds extensively. Hill said that when two people get together, a third mind is created. It was a separate force that came into the conversation with an energetic and perhaps spiritual connotation. He also stated, and he felt strongly about, "Maintain perfect harmony between yourself and every member of your mastermind group. If you fail to carry out this instruction to the letter, expect to meet with failure. The mastermind principle cannot obtain where perfect harmony does not prevail."

The main focus of a mastermind is the brainstorming, accountability, and support of each of the members. It is not about a group coaching session. It is about members sharing with each other so that you can get everyone's feedback and support.

They should be designed so that individuals can get personal attention, brainstorming problem solving, and also accountability with the power of the group. Even a small group of very ambitious, like-minded people, pushing each other forward, can potentially be a huge help to you as an individual trying to grow your business.

Again, the *keys to the kingdom* are when you get your advertising to the point that if you spend a dollar, you get more than a dollar back. At that point, you can start to scale your business potentially without limits. When advertising becomes profitable, it becomes a game changer.

How well you create your lead magnet and information can make a dramatic effect on your conversions.

For example, if 100 people click on your ad, and 10 people take your lead magnet, entering their e-mail, and then two people actually purchase your subsequent product, you now have a 2% conversion rate.

If you have 100 people going to your site, and your advertising costs are $200, but you got the two people to convert at $400 each, now you have a $600 return on $200 invested.

What is the next most logical thing to do?

Spend more. When you get to this level, that's when the entire game changes, and you can infinitely scale your business.

When a system is dialed in and working correctly, it is automated and consistently generates new leads, clients, and cash flow. Once the systems and processes are automated, it becomes kind of like a money tap. Turn it on when you want leads and income... turn it off when you have enough to handle.

Some of the best marketers and business owners in the world are using this exact formula to scale their business. They tweak and adjust and test, with a vengeance, to improve their conversions all the time.

This is how professional marketers are able to scale businesses. This is regardless if its a brick and mortar business or strictly online marketing. They turn marketing into a profitable and consistent flow of new leads, clients and sales. It is created to deliver your ideal message to your perfect client, the client that you would love to work with every day. The power of transforming business marketing into a predictably profitable investment creates the potential for exponential and perhaps unlimited growth.

Facebook™ wants people to stay on their platform. When the Facebook™ algorithm sees a post with lots of engagement it says, "Hey, people like this post lets push it further for more people to see." They want people staying on their platform as long as possible.

The problem for many marketing companies is they are limited by the rest of the business marketing system that the company has created. It's not designed with a strategy to generate consistent growth through lead generation profitably. They may be getting a few people to 'like posts.' As someone said, "You can't eat likes" sums it up quite well.

Many business owners think they know more about how to market than the marketing agencies. The good agencies get through to the owners of the value they bring and the profit the company can make.

To begin your advertising, it doesn't have to cost a lot a $5 -$10 can grow your reach, allow you to reach more clients, and allow your business to grow if you have a system in place to capture leads. This is the step that marketers search and reach for.

When everything is created, tested and launched and aligns correctly and the first sale comes in, then the second, the third and so on. A strategy followed constantly by one of the best at this is they spend $100 to test the ad to see if it converts. If it doesn't they kill the ad and try again.

Once you know the ads are converting you begin to scale your adverting to reach more people for your product or service.

If you look at magazines, newspapers or ads on TV you'll notice that most large companies have not clued into social media yet.

The advertising landscape will change when major companies clue in and start advertising on social. You still have time to get your business up and get advertising at a very economical price now.

Again, you can find more information at www.M5SMareting.com

You're up and running, in the next chapter learn how to sell without selling anything.

Chapter 8

Sales without Selling- a Transformation of Processes

The 4 Secrets to Automating Sales with Maximum Impact

— — — — — — — —

**"What you get by achieving your goals is not as important as
what you become by achieving your goals."**
Zig Ziglar

— — — — — — — —

Did you know that when Carnival Cruise Lines began all of their advertising, they had pictures taken from one side of the ship? The other side was hidden because they did not have the money to finish painting. Carnival was almost out of money and had no real capital. They had to get creative to find the money.

So what did Carnival do?

They traded empty cabins and trips to radio and television stations for advertising. They traded advertising for more trips, to newspapers and magazines, over a ten-year period. Each of the advertisers could provide free trips as bonuses to their employees. The cost of an empty cabin was basically nothing. They charged them only a small processing fee of $90 to book a trip.

This small amount paid for all meals and any other costs of the cabin, plus guests would spend money in the bar, casino, and on gifts.

This strategy allowed Carnival continuous advertising in 100 cities for 10 years, without spending a penny.

It was estimated at millions in advertising, and hundreds of millions in sales, for basically no cost to the cruise lines. It also propelled them to become the largest cruise line in the world. The owner became a billionaire from this form of bartering for services.

Bootstrapping is also a creative name for finding the funding or starting a company without capital. Start researching major companies that had to bootstrap their way to launching, to see if it can help your business.

You are not selling your product or service. You transition to creating packages that you have created. You're selling the benefits of the product or service you provide for your clients.

Even when crap is hitting the fan around the world, the first thing most companies do is scale back their advertising, because they consider it an expense. Most do not understand that there is a science behind marketing. Some of the most dramatic marketing is so simple and with only a few words. There is also a science behind sales.

David Ogilvy is widely known as the father of advertising. He was a founder of Ogilvy & Mather, and passed away in 1999. One of his campaigns made Dove the top selling soap in the United States, and it is still running to this day: "Only Dove is one-quarter moisturizing cream." Another example was for Rolls-Royce: "At 60 mph, the loudest noise in this new Rolls Royce is the electric clock." His advertising resulted in billions of dollars in sales, and cost companies pennies on the dollar.

One of his principles in particular was, "The function of advertising is to sell, and the successful advertising for any product is based on information about its consumer." Know your customer, do your homework on your Avatar, and know them as well or better than they know themselves.

He also believed that the best way to get new clients is by "doing notable work for existing clients." Over deliver every aspect of your services for customers.

Ogilvy followed four basic principles that still apply today:

- Creative brilliance – with a strong emphasis on the "big idea."

- Research – never underestimate the importance of research in advertising.

- Gain actual results for clients – "In the modern world of business, it is useless to be creative unless you could also sell what you create."

- Professional discipline – "I prefer the discipline of knowledge to the anarchy of ignorance."

Look at and research different industries, and adopt and borrow. Some common strategies in other industries are as common as dirt, and are totally normal. These techniques could bring so much power to your business. How are they doing it, and how can you do it also?

There are numerous impact points that existing business owners can use, with minimal investment to create more income, such as:

- Reaching out to clients that they haven't talked to in a long time.

- Initiating a strategic referral system.

- Exploring the profiles of buyers, and their needs that you may not have considered. Look for other opportunities, like a side gig income, that you never considered.

I've been in sales since 2008, since the company I worked at closed down. There is a statement that I found many years ago: "How to do sales without being salesy."

In the many sales training environments I have been in, it has been stated to "Go for the close." Good salespeople are pros; they know the answers to the questions, and the scripts to reply to almost every question you could throw at them. They don't get all sales of course, yet they convert a lot.

In every real estate training I was in they told you to 'cold call' people. For every 100 calls you will get 1 or 2 interested sellers or buyers. The vast majority of agents hate doing cold calls more than the people on the receiving end. Yet it works and their next job is to convert them into clients.

There is another training and system that is sold to Realtors® that you may be familiar with. "I will sell your house guaranteed or I will buy it myself." This is a packaged system designed by an agent that he sells to other agents.

This is based on direct response marketing.

For my first attempt at a short book, I am trying to provide value and information, and to help people perhaps find another way. The hardest part is getting all this information out to your future and prospective clients.

But many people might have a hard time grasping that it starts with one—your perfect client, your Avatar—and delivering your message so that it's just like they wrote it themselves.

Once you have your message created and online, it will live on, giving your business a chance that every single piece created can drive more traffic to your business or service.

Sometimes getting money from the banks to grow your business, without exhausting every other avenue, might be a mistake. How many ways can you generate other revenue streams to your business, with your existing clients and systems you already have in place?

Can you find a complementary product to your "Big Mac," such as adding "fries and a coke?" Add to your offer, and improve the average sale price by 10% or even more.

Put a professional strategy in place to gain referrals from clients, and to also help improve your sales. Someone referring a friend to your business is the easiest sale to make—you already have credibility.

Going back to the story about the psychologist, Jill, she was able to dramatically increase her income, and work with more clients while working far less, by transferring her business online, working "one with many" instead of one on one. Yet she's still able to obtain the same results for her clients; perhaps in some cases, far better. For example, on a group call, the client will realize that they are not alone, and that there are other people going through the same thing. This can potentially give them peace of mind; every case would be different.

Moving forward Jill now decides to create a free webinar or training: "The top 10 things you need to know about releasing your stress during the lockdown and come out of this stronger." Then she created a marketing campaign to advertise to her ideal target market.

- Assume 100 people sign up , and 20 show up; this is a 20% show-up rate. That's 100 people that joined her e-mail database, to whom she can market her products or services later.

- Of the 20 that showed up, assume 10% joined; that's two new clients and a pay day of almost $2,600 less advertising costs.

97

- During the next few days, her webinar plays automatically when people want to watch it, and she gets another two people signing up for another $2,600—a total of $52,400 for the week.

- She makes a few modifications to the webinar after seeing where people drop off. On her next live event, she now converts at 20%, or 4 new clients, and makes $45,200; plus, she enrolls 2 in her high-end offer, which is a more personal one-on-one offer. Can you see the potential?

In this example, the sales can all be completed online with only a payment processor. She is giving away so much value in her "10 things" report, that she has people pre-sold and ready to work with her.

On the sales page, it is just a matter of people entering their information and credit card number to become a paid client. There is no one-on-one talking required to get the sale. Creating a higher price point, up from her premium program, may require one-on-one sales calls.

To make it even more convenient, she adds a booking calendar to her website, where potential customers sign up to book a call.

When it comes to the sales process, this is an art in itself. It is not about the product, the service, or even the information. It is getting clear on communicating the benefits, with the transformation of someone's issues, and solving their problem. What is the benefit to them? What is the cost of not solving their issues?

There are even opportunities for start-up businesses. They can reach more people and have more eyeballs in front of their marketing. To improve their existing business, they could change their marketing, their results, the names of their marketing items, the action steps throughout, and the risk, as well as to offer guarantees, learn how to measure the effectiveness of their marketing, and so much more.

The transformation of someone's life by the solving of a major problem, is the most dramatic effect that coaches, service providers, professionals, consultants, and business owners can provide.

Only one part of the process is marketing and educating people about your product and service. Your marketing can bring in hundreds of people to look, but if this does not result in sales, there is a problem.

Remember the "Big Mac" story; you need the "fries," and to add in the "coke" too. Don't just sell a product—sell a package, your service, your guarantees, and the experience you create. It is also your ability to relay the information regarding the cost to the customer of not solving it.

For a relationship coach, the value they provide in being able to save a marriage rather than a couple going through a divorce, can be profound. If someone has been trying to lose weight, and you are able to help them achieve that goal, how much is that worth?

They feel better, they live longer, and they have all the benefits that go with losing that weight. For the home hobbyist that wants to scrapbook, a small $37 fee is convenient and packed with great tips.

For a business owner that does not have their marketing dialed in, if a marketing program could literally transform a company from doing half a million in sales a year, to a million in sales a year, what is that worth?

For most people being able to replace their income with an extra few thousand dollars a month is life-changing. To transform a business and the impact on the lives and security of the employees and the owner is profound.

Once the process is set up and running, it's rinse, test, and repeat. This is NOT selling a service such as, "I will build you a website," or "I will look after your social media," or "I am a psychologist working with people with depression."

This is selling the outcome, the results, and the transformation that the service provides, to dramatically impact somebody's life and future.

In almost all sales, you are going to have the same concerns, questions, delays, and any other reasons for the potential buyer to not buy. It is human nature to say no. They may need a little help in making up their mind. If your product or service is right for them, and you know it will help, is it not in their best interest to say yes and buy?

Examples are: "I need to think about it"; "I need to talk to my wife/husband"; "I need to check our finances"; "It's not the right time"; "I need to talk to my business partner." If the decision maker is not there, why do the presentation? You would just have to do it again, if you break through the barrier to finally get to see them again.

Typically, there will not be that many reasons for them to say no. Identify all of the reasons that someone might say no, prior to getting into the sales conversation.

Write down the logical reasons why their concerns are unfounded, and answer with a well-thought-out and logical answer. Test every time, and confidently address the concerns during your presentation. Work toward increasing the chances of pre-selling your clients, by addressing their concerns before they are even aware of many of them.

I listened to a story a while ago about how a guy did a sales presentation on stage, and he ended up with absolutely no sales. He was crushed and went and hid in his room for quite a while. Someone else that sold his training program to numerous people at the same event, took him out to dinner.

While they were talking, this guy kept asking him question after question. He was establishing a pattern of him saying yes. This could be vocally or the client just agreeing internally and saying yes repeatedly.

This is a psychological strategy; once people are used to saying yes repeatedly, it becomes easier to get the yes for the sale. It all has to make sense; people are smart, and you need to crush their objections logically. A few years later in 2019 this same guy closed a record $3,000,000 in sales in 90 minutes. This I share more of in the bonuses at www.M5SMarketing.com

The beautiful thing about creating a treasure trove of your own articles that you can deploy whenever you like, is that you are pre-selling consumers. The ones that continue to follow your articles get to know, like, and trust you, and want to work with you. Online sales can be completed by credit card. This is when you can make money while you sleep.

Consider again the example of Tom. People had to apply, and he has the credentials to get the results. It can reverse the sales process to ultimately having clients pre-sold on your services, and searching you out.

It is a matter of both being sold on wanting to work with each other. Isn't this a much easier and nicer way to sell? Sometimes people discover you, but they may be years out from purchasing. This is why you create your e-mail list.

Your advertising is always being tested for better conversions. Your landing pages are being split tested. You have your initial sales message recorded, designed to draw in your ideal clients. The marketing pieces you have created raise their objections in their minds, and you crush the objections logically. Each part of the marketing and logic is designed to get clients to say yes.

When someone signs up on your e-mail list, the thank you page is where you can absolutely outshine all your competitors. It is the one e-mail that has the highest open rate of all. Your e-mail system automatically sends them your welcome message, which is your most important e-mail. Welcome new people to your list, tell them what to do next, and reassure them that they are in safe hands.

Be sure to visit www.M5SMarketing.com to get your bonuses and more details.

Chapter 9

Stability, Then the "Keys to the Kingdom" for Growth

The 6 Steps to Building a Money Tap for Growth

————————

*"Whether you think you can, or you
think you can't, you're right."*
~Henry Ford~

————————

You may have watched the movie, *Catch Me if You Can*, with Leonardo DiCaprio and Tom Hanks, which was released in 2002. For those of you that haven't, it's a true story based on the life of Frank Abagnale.

 When he was a teenager, Frank started a life of crime, beginning when his parents divorced. He needed money for survival, and began by forging Pan-Am Airline payroll checks. He traveled the world for free and, at the same time, was cashing millions of dollars in checks. He was actually caught by the FBI. He conned his way out, and escaped by convincing the agent that he was CIA.

Frank went on to impersonate a doctor, a lawyer, and a teacher. He fell in love with a girl who had an attorney as a father, and asked her father for permission to marry her. Her father also helped him in taking the Louisiana state bar exam, which Frank actually passed.

It was here, though, that the FBI almost caught up with them. Frank asked Brenda, his fiancée, to meet him at the airport and escape. Frank sees cops everywhere and knows right away that she betrayed him. He slipped onto a plane and made his escape to Europe.

He was finally caught in a small town in France, and was sentenced to 12 years in a maximum-security prison in the US. Frank got early release by working for the FBI bank fraud unit. He became a security expert in finding counterfeiters.

Part of the story was that Frank also taught as a teacher at Brigham Young University. When he was caught, one of the things that the FBI was very curious about and asked him was how he was able to teach a university class. Frank replied, "I would read one chapter ahead." The university will still not acknowledge that he deceived them and was able to teach their university students.

Even though you might not be an expert yet at what you would love to do, you need to be determined to become the expert through your journey.

Don't make claims that you can't fulfill. Dive in and learn more. Ask your potential clients what they need. How can you help? Keep your mind open to the possibilities of pivoting in a new direction with your business.

Ask questions and listen to what people say.

Learn something new, and even if you think you can't do it, turn it around and have faith in yourself, and say, "I can do this." This is perhaps where the saying comes back, "Who, not how." It's not *how* you can do it; it's *who* can do it for you.

Tony Robbins is probably the most well-known and famous coaches in the world. Everything described in this book, about websites, funnels, content, advertising, products, and coaching, is being done by Tony Robbins. You can find out more by using Google and searching for Tony Robbins' funnel. He has four stages:

Lead magnet: Tony's lead magnets are usually low-cost or zero, such as his videos, his reports, TV shows, YouTube, and Facebook™; much of this is just building brand awareness.

Tripwire: These are his books, such as *Awaken the Giant Within*, and courses, such as Personal Power. These are typically low cost and affordable for the average person to help build awareness around his brand.

Core product: His events are priced from around $1,000 to around $25,000. If you follow Tony Robbins, you will see how many people are at these events.

Profit multiplier: His Platinum Partnership business coaching program costs from around $65,000 to $150,000.

Does this look familiar?

Get out of your head and connect with others that are like you. At this time, you cannot go to live events, but you can still connect with extremely smart folks anywhere in the world. You can find a group online, for almost anything you can imagine.

Scared about trying something new?

The fear you have of going after your dream is imaginary. Break down the walls and reach outside your comfort zone. Start with the end in mind, a three-year plan, but it's the next 30 days that are critical. It's just like planning your next amazing vacation when this is all over.

You plan where you're going, and all the great things you will do, see, and experience. You will also plan on how to get there the fastest, safest, and most efficient way possible.

Get clear on your vision. What are your goals, your ambitions, your dreams, and your desires, and what are you willing to do to get there?

When I heard this quote, it was kind of profound: "Stability is wrong." If a company is stable, it's not growing. Many times, a business owner will try to find more capital to invest in the business.

A quick question to ask is, "If your business was a mutual fund, would you buy it?" If you're investing in a mutual fund, today you hope for a return of 5%, would love 8-10%, and freak out with happiness if you got 15% consistently.

Popular magazines have major business brands dominating advertising, and these companies spend a fortune. Smaller magazines have sections where many smaller companies advertise, and the costs are still prohibitively expensive. This advertising is extremely hard, if not impossible, with the setup to track the ROI (return on investment).

It doesn't take much to research websites that smaller companies have, if they have one at all. Check out their social media presence. There are so many businesses that need help. Many do not even have a modern website.

Most, if they have a website, are not effective at gaining leads. If you do not have a business yet, consider what would happen if you learned how to build a professional marketing system.

Complete the writing of your "10 things" report, and get it professionally edited and styled. Also have the e-book completed into

10 separate reports. Would this put you one step ahead of your competitors?

Look in the mirror; this is your competitor.

There are many companies offering the software to create your funnel. When the top of your funnel is created, this is where you drive all your traffic. The first part of the M5 process is to understand how to create your content. Getting the basics of your funnel set up and operational is the next most important thing now.

- Your free report is available to download instantly by entering their e-mail.

- You have your autoresponder series, and e-mails are ready to go.

- You have a thank you page created, with an offer to help.

- You perhaps have an order form.

- You have a webinar registration page, and directions to another page in your funnel.

- You have a payment processor set up for people that want to complete a purchase right away.

This is the setup of a marketing system that can create an incredible income every year in business. You've already created the lead magnet that you can share through numerous channels. There is no limit to both offline and online strategies to reach more people.

People like to learn different ways: Some like to read, some like to listen, and others like to watch video. Take one chapter from your report, such as, "The 3 things to know about...," and create a video, teaching people.

You can live-stream your information, set it up so that it's streamed on other channels, and have it recorded to play later in other locations.

You can have it transcribed into print so that you can create new reports.

You now have a video on YouTube and on Facebook; you have the audio for a podcast, and you have a printed version that people can download—and every one of these can drive people back to your landing page.

You create the next piece of content, and repeat the process, doing the same thing. Ask people what they like about the content, and what else they would like to know. They help create your content; you never run out of content to help your clients or just to help people.

If you produce a professional webinar that you run every week, and it is converting into leads and sales every time you run it, how much could this be worth for your business?

You have the e-book, the 10 reports, the 10 videos, the 10 audios, the 10 podcast subjects, and the 10-step e-mail system to share with the world. Every week, you can create new and unique content for those who join your list.

It doesn't matter whether you are in the brick and mortar business world, or if you are online creating content. Everyone is consuming tons of content right now; at this time, this may be the best way to increase your reach for business, now and into the future.

There are so many businesses that constantly blast out "we have the best price." It's almost a race to the bottom. I guarantee that they do not have the best service, the follow-up, or the package that will absolutely wow their customers.

It's a product at bare bones, kind of like Walmart.

Do you want your business bouncing around and competing with the bottom of the barrel, or do you want to set yourself apart to be the best and the most expensive...and for a reason. Set yourself apart with excellence in everything you do.

Jay Abraham's strategy of preeminence is about positioning your product or service, and providing an outstanding package, as well as solving your clients' needs, and going further by solving problems that they didn't even know they had.

You become exceptional and outstanding, with a "wow factor" that truly resonates with your clients. When businesses look closely at what their competitors are doing, many realize that it may not be that hard to excel.

The last step in growing, is scaling your business.

You can create teams to help in aspects to free up your time, or you can keep going, just yourself. Chances are, if you have completed the journey, you will want to help more people and make more money. All your pre-conceived beliefs are gone, but now you have a whole new set of them. Imposter syndrome is so common when people launch. Rest assured...you are not alone.

Be sure to visit www.M5SMarketing.com to get your bonuses.

Chapter 10

Scaling – The Power of Growth with Social Media and a System

A Million Dollar a Year Company – How the Pros Do It

————————
"Whenever you find yourself on the side of the majority,
it's time to pause and reflect."
~Mark Twain~
————————

Rather than build one part of a course that leaves more pieces of the puzzle for my clients to figure out, I wanted to get it all into packages, into a process and it started with this book.

From here, and with the bonuses at www.M5Smarketing.com, my goal is to create a complete system that gains results. Today, information is cheap; it's everywhere. You can learn anything you want just by going online and researching.

What is in short supply are true transformation systems and processes. That is my goal for my clients with the M5S System: to transform their marketing process into a profitable system.

We need to transition to the talk about internet millionaires.

People that have not experienced this world do not have the understanding of how this is created. The fact is, with over 7 billion people on the planet, there is no shortage of people to market your products . You only need a very few to increase your company size and reach this level.

"How to build a chicken coop" has made millions using the same strategies that have been presented. The owner of "Bigfoot Hunting Trips" booked thousands of dollars in pre-paid trips for hunters. Yes, that's correct; Bigfoot doesn't exist (well, at least no one has proved it), and people booked these trips.

What you create online doesn't necessarily have to be about business. It can be based on a hobby, or something you love. You do need to make sure there is a market for it. Don't try to reinvent the wheel. Do your research online, and find somebody else that has done something similar. Buy that person's course, and drastically improve it with your own personal touches and voice.

Transform your mindset to the 100% belief that anything is possible. What if you killed the beliefs that are keeping you in the state of scarcity—the language and the stories we tell ourselves every day?

You have to change your beliefs. You actually may have to change your identity. In these days, it might help just to protect your sanity.

Question: What would be another word for marriage counsellor? How about a coach? The story of Gulliver—what do you think he does? He does classes, and they do coaching. I told you the example of Jill, the psychologist—is she doing coaching? It might be called a different name at times, but basically, it is all coaching.

There's a massive difference between a course and actual coaching. I can't remember who I heard this from, but it went like this: "The poor have the government to protect them; successful people hire coaches to help them become more successful; and the middle class don't believe in them—they have no one."

How do you want to be positioned when we come out of this?

How do you want to position your company, your business, and your life while we're in the midst of this?

How would it feel knowing that once you have created your marketing system, you never have to worry about getting new clients ever again?

What if you could take your passion, skill set, your experience, or your business, and set your business up to grow faster than most people dream of? This is in good times, let alone these uncertain times.

What would it feel like, knowing that you've finally cracked the code on how professional marketers are still able to create sales even in times like this?

Don't think outside the box; right now, there is no box. Go after, do, or create whatever you want, provided there is a market.

These steps are the same steps that have essentially been explained throughout this book. You can set up a brand new business, or you can make the choice to re-establish your business marketing right now. The steps are the same for all industries. This is the power of marketing.

The 4 Key Steps:

- Know your target market, unpack your knowledge, deliver your expertise, and get paid for the transformation you provide. When you put yourself and your company directly in front of your clients consistently, your business game and results will start to change.

- It must be you or a key player that creates the *initial* marketing articles. No one loves or is as invested in your business as much as you.

- Understanding the "process" allows you to create and offer new products, services, and new information, and even enter brand new markets fast.

- Once you gain clarity of the system, you can hire out the work to more seasoned professionals, and have greater control over strategy.

Carefully crafted messages are designed to result in more leads, conversions, and sales for your business. When the marketing begins, it does take work and testing; however, once your offer is dialed in and successfully converting, it can run almost on autopilot.

The key is to test, test, test, test...

What it takes to create a million dollar a year company? It may be easier to understand by breaking it down into much simpler terms.

- A million dollar a year business is one that makes $83,333 per month.

- A million dollar a year business is one that makes $19,231 per week.

- Based on an 8-hour workday, and 20 days a month, a million dollar a year business is one that makes around $480 per hour.

Does Jill's have the potential of being a million dollar per year business? Does Tom's? Does Mike's?

The chart below explains the costs and number of sales for someone to reach the 7 figure per year level. I added both one-time sales and membership sites.

	One-Time Sales			Membership Site	
Consumer Price	Buyers	Per Month		Monthly Cost	Active Members
$100	10,000	833		$27	3086
$250	4,000	334		$40	2083
$750	1,333	111		$85	980
$1,000	1,000	84		$170	490
$1,500	667	56		$350	238
$5,000	200	17		$1,000	83
$20,000	50	4.2		$2,000	42

Remember the John Reece story? He gained 1000 new clients with a $1,000 product, and made a million in 24 hours. Taking this into a year, he has to sell 84 a month, or around 3 a day. A membership site like Mike's, with 2,083 clients paying $40 a month, is a million dollars per year.

The process is a system and can be duplicated.. You can mix low ticket and high ticket, and a variety of other services, into the packages you create. Remember, this is just one part of the game. You are providing a service to your customers; except now, with your new marketing, you're gaining more customers. Perhaps you're expanding your business market to entirely new markets and new opportunities.

Looking at the examples above, ask yourself: "How much is the cost of opportunity?

Welcome to the game...

...You are already in it.

The 4 Rules of the Game

Your Character: Upon learning the rules of the new game, move into momentum, every day, taking one step forward. When you push forward and continue the process, you will not be the same person you are today. Who will you help? What will you do? Who will you become?

Your Goal: Open your mind to the endless possibilities that are out there. Put aside all the lies you tell yourself that are not true. Get rid of your limiting beliefs. Ignore the opinions of others that have no business telling you anything. It's your life and dreams, not theirs.

The Enemy: Continuing your life and accepting the status quo. Stop listening to doubters, naysayers, and critics, and to the fear of starting something new. Stop listening to the biggest of all critics...your ego, the voice inside your head. Time is a resource of which we all have equal amounts, and only a limited amount. Stop wasting it.

Your Allies: Work, connect, and network with others that will become your allies, cheerleaders, and friends. Remember that you are closer to absolutely anyone in the world than you have ever been before.

We will come out of this pandemic, but some businesses will be closed forever. Some will just hang on, and when the economy restarts, they will still just be hanging on. Then there are others that will invest in learning, building, and creating something more. They will have established a goal to reach for, and are moving toward it every day, one step at a time.

The Final Steps to Moving Ahead...

Everyone starts at the very beginning...the biggest thing is to start.
"I've had a great deal of troubles in my life,
most of which have never happened."
~Mark Twain~

This part is to help you understand, with a bit of clarity, your dream—your dream of what you want. Close your eyes and think about your perfect ideal day, and answer these questions.

Where would you wake up? Where would you live? Who do you wake up with? Are you in the same house, in another home, or a much bigger home? Is it the same city, in the country, or even the same country? Feel this like you're there and not imagining it! Use all of your senses...feel it, touch it, taste the flavors of the food, and smell the scents in the air. Live it in your mind, with the reality that you have already achieved your goal.

What will you have for breakfast? What will you do in the morning, and who with? What would you have for lunch? Where would you have lunch? Would you have a business meeting? Would you be with your spouse, kids, or with your friends or family? What would you do in the afternoon? Where would you go out for supper? Would you have dinner at home or dinner out with friends?

Take 30 minutes right now; think about this, and write down your perfect day. Don't date this; put it into your wallet or purse, and just remember that it is there. Believe with all your heart and mind that you already have achieved it. Reinforce it by reminding yourself that you have already achieved it, and the steps you take today will help you get there faster.

Here are a few more steps:

- Make the decision right now to create your dream board, your 35,000,000-foot view; something you can look at every single day to remind you.

- Create your personal affirmation chant to positively reinforce your thinking. Start rewiring your beliefs that anything is possible.

- Fight negativity. The negativity that's all around us will always try to break through.

- When your ego sows you doubt, shut it off by reading your affirmations.

- Find a community of people that have dreams as big as or bigger than yours.

Make the decision that absolutely nothing is going to stop you! Find the power to push forward every single day to gain your own momentum, from a pebble to a boulder, rolling down a hill. Push yourself out of your comfort zone.

If you did this every day, can you imagine how you'll change in a year?

Start today, right now...

...take this time and use it to your advantage.

Go to www.M5SMarketing.com for your free bonuses, and much more information.

About the Author

Peter Rollings was born in Brockville, a small town on the St. Lawrence River, at the start of the Thousand Islands, in Ontario. His dad passed away in 1980, when he was 17, which resulted in him, his brother, Jack, and his sister, Karen, being split up. A few months later, he needed a job and started working in the same factory that his dad had worked at. He worked there for 27 years, until free trade resulted in the company moving to Mexico.

This started his journey into the business and marketing world. He attempted to start a large company right after being let go. He got so close, yet it never launched. He also got his real estate license in 2008, and he learned to code and build websites in 2009. Due to his frustration in working with other companies that never quite delivered what was promised, he learned to build websites that gained thousands of visitors, every month, for free. He realized although essential, this is the long game, and always thought that there must be a better way. He also discovered that he hated coding.

It was one online purchase from a professional internet marketer in 2014 that changed his course. He understood what he wanted to be able to do. He needed the next pieces of the puzzle. For the next 6 years, he continued to take courses, go to events, and meet people that were playing this marketing game on a totally different level.

"I wanted a system that takes the very best information, and transform a difficult puzzle into one that can be learned and created fast, to be able to get my clients results." His goal is to "help business owners, even start-ups, to create their marketing systems so that they can grow more, profit more, and at the same time, create far more free time for themselves."

In his coaching business, he strives to get his clients to first understand the big view of their goals. Many times, a client have problems that they never considered, which causes a world of stress. They have to break it down into shorter timelines, bite-size chunks, and to address them with each part building on the other. The result is creating a map of the system that his clients understand and implement.

There is one critical aspect that he wants to share with you,...

"This is a journey, have fun with it. Don't loose sight the things that are great in your life right now. Simple things that we take for granted that we so often fail to appreciate. If you think that life will be better when you reach your goal, whatever it may be, don't miss the great moments along the way. The truth is when you reach your goal you may be disappointed and start striving for the next one. Be grateful for everything you have in your life right now everyday and simply have fun working towards your goals. Celebrate small achievements, smile, laugh, get around people that are positive. Life is to short be sucked into negativity.

If you are interested in working with Peter reach out to him at his website www.M5SMarketing.com.

Peter has three children, Rhiannon, Katherine, and James, who have all become amazing young adults. When not working, you can find him... well, maybe you can't, because he loves the water and outdoors, and loves to get away and disappear "off the grid," several times a year.

www.M5SMarketing.com

www.ingramcontent.com/pod-product-compliance
Lightning Source LLC
Chambersburg PA
CBHW072157090426
42740CB00012B/2303